Knowledge Infrastructure and Higher Education in India

This short book examines the availability and adoption of new education technologies in higher education institutions in India. It provides a summary of the activities in which such technologies are being used and the catalytic factors for such adoptions. The book also evaluates the impact on skill development, and will be a useful reference for those who are interested to find out more about technology adoption and implementation in higher education, and what the challenges are through the learning experiences in these education institutions.

Kaushalesh Lal is Professor at the Society for Development Studies, New Delhi and a Professorial Fellow at United Nations University – Maastricht Economic and Social Research Institute on Innovation and Technology (UNU-MERIT), Maastricht.

Shampa Paul is Associate Professor at the Society for Development Studies, New Delhi.

Routledge Focus on Economics and Finance

The fields of economics are constantly expanding and evolving. This growth presents challenges for readers trying to keep up with the latest important insights. Routledge Focus on Economics and Finance presents short books on the latest big topics, linking in with the most cutting-edge economics research.

Individually, each title in the series provides coverage of a key academic topic, whilst collectively the series forms a comprehensive collection across the whole spectrum of economics.

Microfinance
Research, Debates, Policy
Bernd Balkenhol

The Malaysian Banking Industry
Policies and Practices after the Asian Financial Crisis
Rozaimah Zainudin, Chan Sok Gee and Aidil Rizal Shahrin

Automation, Capitalism and the End of The Middle Class
Jon-Arild Johannessen

Cryptocurrencies
A Primer on Digital Money
Mark Grabowski

Knowledge Infrastructure and Higher Education in India
Kaushalesh Lal and Shampa Paul

For a full list of titles in this series, please visit www.routledge.com/Routledge-Focus-on-Economics-and-Finance/book-series/RFEF

Knowledge Infrastructure and Higher Education in India

Kaushalesh Lal and Shampa Paul

LONDON AND NEW YORK

First published 2020
by Routledge
2 Park Square, Milton Park, Abingdon, Oxon OX14 4RN

and by Routledge
52 Vanderbilt Avenue, New York, NY 10017

Routledge is an imprint of the Taylor & Francis Group, an informa business

British Library Cataloguing-in-Publication Data
A catalogue record for this book is available from the British Library

Library of Congress Cataloging-in-Publication Data
A catalog record has been requested for this book

ISBN: 978-0-367-42328-5 (hbk)
ISBN: 978-0-367-82357-3 (ebk)

Typeset in Times New Roman
by Wearset Ltd, Boldon, Tyne and Wear

To all those who contribute to the development of educational technologies

Contents

Figures

Tables

Foreword

The developing world has witnessed an unprecedented increase in the participation of private sector in higher education in recent times. The main reason for the surge in private sector investment is the inability of governments to keep pace with technological development, greater demand of higher education institutions and infrastructure needed for such institutions. Consequently, governments around the world are encouraging the participation of the private sector in the field of education. While allowing it to function under broad policy guidelines of the government, private sector institutions have been encouraged and incentivized to upgrade technological and physical infrastructure.

There are barriers to the adoption of New Educational Technologies (NET) for the benefit of students; the most critical being that NET are costly and may not be economically viable for the private sector. The opposite view on the adoption of NET in private institutions is that such institutions are expected to adopt NET due to competitive pressure from challenging institutions. Another factor that determines faster adoption of new technologies is the acquisition procedure, which is very simple in private organizations and depends largely on the disposition of the owner of the institution. On the other hand, the archaic and bureaucratic procedure of technology acquisition in public-funded institutions tend to cause substantial delays in the adoption of new technologies. There are several other factors which may result in varying degree of NET use in private and public-funded institutions.

This is a very timely book that examines the adoption of NET in both public and private institutions. It is especially important in an era of Industry 4.0 (The Fourth Industrial Revolution) with the attendant emergence of new techniques such as Cloud Computing, Artificial Intelligence (AI), big data analytics, Robotics and Process Automation (RPA) among others. Another distinguishing aspect of the book is the in-depth coverage of the two critical domains of society: public-funded and privately owned institutions.

The coverage includes a wide array of technologies from standalone computers to online teaching. The robustness of the findings is strengthened by the use of appropriate econometric and statistical techniques deployed by the authors. The methodology enriches the analysis that is substantiated by the inclusion of views of all the stakeholders in higher education. Although the book presents empirical evidence from Higher Education Institutions (HEI) in India, it offers clear and important lessons for other countries.

The book covers not only the degree of adoption of NET but also analyses the impact of such technologies on students and how these technologies are helping teachers in managing their activities digitally. The analysis of skill creation among students from the use of NET is a unique contribution of the study. The book also covers to what extent the use of NET fosters graduate employment.

Policy makers will have substantive lessons on the differentiated nature of public and private financing; for example, there is clear evidence that the degree of adoption of NET varies between self-financed and public-funded institutions. The role of management plays a catalytic factor in adoption and effective use of NET in self-financed institutions. The role of management is found to be imperative not only in faster acquisition of NET but also in motivating teachers to use it effectively.

The NET encompasses two constituents, namely, technologies within the control of the management and, second, those that are beyond control of the institutions. For instance the provision of high bandwidth is under the control of the government and not within the institutions. The book therefore recommends availability of widespread, high speed, effective and efficient communication network and to upgrade it on a regular basis.

This is an important addition to the field of digital education. I believe the book will be of tremendous benefit to all stakeholders in higher education including students, researchers, teachers, policy makers and management.

Professor Banji Oyelaran-Oyeyinka
Senior Special Adviser to President of the
African Development Bank on Industrialization and
Professorial Fellow, United Nations University-MERIT

Acknowledgements

The authors would like to place on record the appreciation of students and faculty of all seven institutions who very willingly shared the information with us. We highly appreciate the encouragement of Prof. Alakh N. Sharma, Director, Institute for Human Development, Delhi. We are grateful to Prof. Shrirang Altekar, Director and Dr Anubha Vashisth, Symbiosis Centre for Management Studies, NOIDA; Prof. M. S. Bhat, Department of Economics, Jamia Millia Islamia University, Delhi; and Prof. C. K. Jaggi, Department of Operational Research, University of Delhi whose support was incredible in conducting the survey of students and faculty of the respective universities. The contributions of Sri Satyendra Kumar, Jawaharlal Nehru University, Delhi; Prof. Sweta Anand and Dr Vidushi Sharma, Gautam Buddha University, NOIDA; Prof. Latika Singh and Dr Tanya Beniwal of Northcap University and Ansal University, Gurugram respectively are thankfully acknowledged. Our thanks are due to Mr Ashwani Jha and Mr S. Sreedharan who very competently carried out the survey and compiled the data. Finally but most importantly, without the financial support of Indian Council of Social Science Research (ICSSR) and the logistic support of Institute for Human Development (IHD), we would not have been able to complete the study.

Abbreviations

ACM	Association for Computing Machinery
AI	Artificial Intelligence
AISHE	All India Survey of Higher Education
BA	Bachelor of Arts
BCom	Bachelor of Commerce
BSc	Bachelor of Science
FDI	Foreign Direct Investment
GBPS	Giga bytes per second
GBU	Gautam Buddha University
HEI	Higher Education Institutions
IBM	International Business Machines Corporation
ICT	Information and Communication Technology
IEEE	Institute of Electrical and Electronics Engineers
IT	Information Technology
JMI	Jamia Millia Islamia
JNU	Jawaharlal Nehru University
LAN	Local Area Network
LMS	e-Learning Management System
MA	Master of Arts
MBPS	Mega bytes per second
MCom	Master of Commerce
MOOC	Massive open online course
MPhil	Master of Philosophy
MSc	Master of Science
NAAC	National Assessment and Accreditation Council
NCR	National Capital Region
NCU	Northcap University
NET	New Educational Technologies
NOIDA	New Okhla Industrial Development Authority
PEOU	Perceived Ease of Use

PhD	Doctor of Philosophy
PISA	Programme for International Students' Assessment
PU	Perceived Usefulness
RPA	Robotics and Process Automation
SCMS	Symbiosis Centre for Management Studies
SIU	Symbiosis International University
TAM	Technology Acceptance Model
TRA	Theory of Reasoned Action
UGC	University Grants Commission
UNESCO	United Nations Educational, Scientific and Cultural Organization

1 Introduction

Education plays a supreme role in the life of an individual. It is a very socially oriented activity and quality education has traditionally been associated with the ability of teachers to communicate with learners effectively. In recent times however teaching methodology has experienced tremendous change. New Educational Technologies (NET) are expected to help both teachers and students. Better quality of education is translated into human capital with skill commensurate with current industrial needs. Modern technologies such as computational and networking technologies have been most remarkable and transformative over the past three decades. The emergence and convergence of these technologies have been termed Information and Communication Technology (ICT). The ICTs specific to educational institutions are termed as NET. It is defined as the combination of computer technology with telecommunications technology. The term includes computer hardware and digital/analogue devices and software applications. NET offers new opportunities and flexibilities but also comes with many challenges.

The integration of latest technology into all facets of education has already become a reality. The integration of new technologies into higher education stimulates several broader innovations. NET-based teaching and learning strategies open possibilities for designing new curricula and new methods of assessment to meet the educational objectives. The use of latest technologies provides universities with flexibility of resources to meet the needs of their students to enhance learning. The growing use of NET is changing and will likely continue to change many of the strategies employed by both teachers and students in the learning processes. The use of NET in education lends itself to the content-centred curricula and competency-based curricula. This leads to more student-centred learning settings. But with the world moving rapidly into digital media and information, the role of NET in education is becoming more and more pivotal and this importance will continue to grow and develop in the twenty-first century. As students and teachers gain access to higher bandwidths, more direct forms of communication and access to sharable resources, the capability to support these quality learning settings will continue to grow (Oliver, 2013). NET by their very nature are tools that encourage and support independent learning. Students using NET for learning purposes, become immersed in the process of learning and more and more students use computers as information sources and cognitive tools (Jonassen & Reeves, 1996). Learning approaches using NET provide many opportunities for constructive learning through their provision and support for resource-based, student-centred settings and by enabling learning to be related to context and to practice (Berge, 1998).

The integration of NET into educational classroom teaching has attained a new upsurge recently. This is marked by inclusion of NET into educational activities run by the academic institutions across the world. NET can be used to promote greater and more efficient communication not only within the institutions but also among them. It would enhance the effectiveness of administration of an educational institution. The ready access to online data and information supports effective decision-making at all levels. Several developing countries including India have witnessed the importance and implications of latest technology in education. In developed countries like the western economy, the Internet and computers are available in the classroom.

It is worth mentioning that pervasiveness of NET is very large. They can be applied in managerial functions in academic institutions or for knowledge acquisition and dissemination among students. There has been rapid adoption of NET in Indian educational institutions, i.e. at school as well as tertiary levels. However, it is less known for what purpose these institutions are using these new technologies. Irrespective of the purpose of the use of NET, a strong and reliable physical and technological infrastructure called knowledge infrastructure is essential for successful use of new technologies. Knowledge infrastructure has two components. First, that which is within control of the institution that intends to adopt NET and second, that which is beyond the limit of individual institutions. The second part of the knowledge infrastructure encompasses a reliable communication network connecting national and international boundaries. Providing latest communication technologies is the responsibility of the state.

The recent literature (Hirakawa et al., 2013; Moretti, 2013; and others) highlights the importance of human capital in economic development. The findings are similar in developing and developed countries. While skilled human capital is needed for adoption of modern technologies in the developing world, innovative human capital is essential for the generation of new ideas and technology in the developed world. In a developing country like India every effort is being made to create skilled human capital. In this context, educational institutions have experienced ICT-led technical change over the last two decades or so. Educational institutions are adopting these new technologies at the school and tertiary level so that students can understand the theoretical concepts in science and mathematics particularly rather than just reproducing the principles in exams without proper understanding. Technologies such as e-classrooms and the Internet have the potential to easily augment the understanding of students.

Skills and knowledge are the driving forces of economic growth and social development for any country. Countries with higher and better levels of skills adjust more effectively to challenges and opportunities. India is progressively moving towards a knowledge economy, due to the abundance of capable, flexible and qualified human capital. Thus, it has become increasingly important that the country should focus on advancement of skills that are relevant to the emerging economic environment. In order to further develop and empower human capital to ensure global competitiveness, it is necessary to impart quality education at the tertiary level. Although emphatic stress is placed on education and training in India, there is still a shortage of skilled manpower to address the mounting needs and demands of the economy.

In view of the pervasiveness of digital technologies, there are so many aspects that can be investigated. However, in order to keep this study focused the objectives are limited. The purpose of this study is to find out the use of NET in higher education from the perspective of all stakeholders i.e. students, teachers and management. It is proposed to carry out a study of tertiary educational institutions in India and the extent and purpose of adoption of NET. This is expected to bring out the trend and pattern of NET adoption. The study will highlight the gaps in adoption of NET compared to what is available globally. The specific objectives of the study are:

a to understand the pattern of adoption of NET in tertiary educational institutions worldwide;
b to examine the availability and adoption of NET at higher educational institutions in India;
c to investigate the gap of adoption of NET in private and state-funded institutions;
d to identify catalytic factors in the adoption of NET;
e to assess the impact of adoption of NET on skill creation among students;
f to identify the impediments to adoption of NET and make recommendations so that students in private and government-aided institutions get the same opportunities for learning.

In view of the above objectives, the following hypotheses are formulated:

- a It is expected that at the higher education level, NET are limited to managerial functions. The adoption of NET in teaching is very limited.
- b Intensity of adoption of NET in private-funded institutions is expected to be more than in government institutions.
- c It is expected that students who are taught through NET are more creative than others.
- d The role of the state is important for diffusion of NET.

The analytical framework depicted in Figure 1.1 has been used in the study. It can be seen from the figure that the extent of NET use is reinforced by several factors. This section discusses the association between use of NET and various factors associated with higher education.

NET has found a significant place in higher education. Its effective use has tremendous potential for enhancing outreach and improving the quality of education. However, there are several factors that reinforce the use of NET. For instance the age of an individual influences the usage of NET. Senior students are expected to use new technologies more than younger

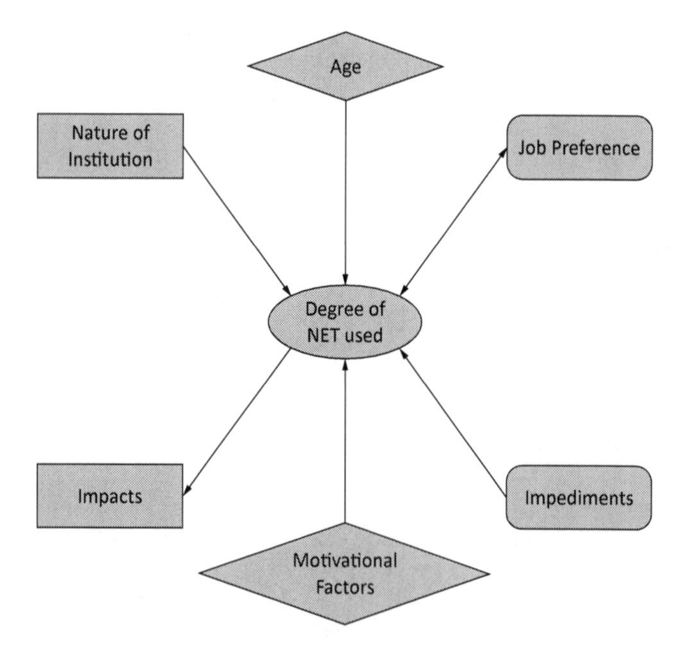

Figure 1.1 Theoretical framework.

students as they need to use digital technologies for their day-to-day research activities. Also they are more acquainted with NET due to easy accessibility and reduced complexity of the new digital technologies. Similarly the younger faculty is expected to be more technology savvy and is aware of the benefits of its use. Hence they are likely to use digital technologies more than senior teachers.

The financial nature of the institution might influence the adoption of new technologies as the private universities face severe competition from others such institutions and government universities. Hence they are expected to be up to date as far as the provision of digital technologies is concerned. They could easily do so as their decision-making process is very simple compared to public-owned institutions. The private institutions could attract more students due to the provision of state-of-the-art new learning technologies. Therefore it is assumed that students studying in private institutions are likely to have access to more advanced digital technologies. Consequently usage of NET by students studying in private institutions is expected to be more extensive. Moreover the management in private institutions can provide incentives to the faculty to use more advanced digital technologies while it is very difficult to provide any kind of incentives in public-funded universities. Therefore the faculty in private-funded universities is likely to use more advanced NET.

The bidirectional arrow between job preference and the degree of NET use indicates both are interdependent as students who would prefer ICT-related jobs are likely to use NET extensively and extensive use of NET would enable them to get jobs in the ICT sector easily. The association between degree of NET use and impediments is depicted by a unidirectional arrow, suggesting that factors such as unreliable technology, insufficient infrastructure, lack of competent faculty etc. are likely to be the impediments in the use of NET by students. The use of NET is unlikely to change the impediments and hence the relationship is unidirectional. NET usage is expected to have some impact on students. Those could be increased creativity, making them more confident, improved learning abilities and providing opportunity to interact with students of other institutions. A unidirectional relationship between use of NET and its impact is assumed.

The motivational factors are very important in both types of institution. However the faculty in private universities can be easily motivated by the management while it is totally dependent on the faculty in public universities to use digital technologies or not. The university administration has little influence in this. So the use of NET is expected to be dependent on the motivation of teachers. As far as the motivational factors related to students are concerned, the adoption of any new technology would not be successful unless the students are willing to learn and appreciate its use.

Various aspects of adoption of NET and its consequences are analysed in the following chapters. Chapter 2 presents the extensive literature survey focusing on NET adoption and its consequences by the institutions located in the developing and developed world. Chapter 3 deals with the opinions of students of these institutions on various aspects of NET. The chapter also presents detailed analysis of students' data. Chapter 4 identifies the factors that have resulted in varying levels of NET use. The chapter has already been published in the *Journal of Educational Technology Systems*. Chapter 5 analyses the data collected from faculty of the institutions covered in the study. The role of management is considered crucial in adoption of NET, and, keeping this aspect of new technologies in mind, the views of management were also collected. The analysis of such views is presented in Chapter 6. Finally, Chapter 7 presents a summary of the study and also policy implications are drawn.

References

Berge, Z. (1998). Guiding principles in web-based instructional design. *Education Media International*, 35(2), 72–76.

Hirakawa, H., Lal, K., Shinkai, N., & Norio, T. (Eds.) (2013). *Servitization, IT-ization and Innovation Models: Two-stage Industrial Cluster Theory*. London and New York: Routledge.

Jonassen, D., & Reeves, T. (1996). Learning with technology: Using computers as cognitive tools. In D. Jonassen (Ed.). *Handbook of Research Educational on Educational Communications and Technology* (pp. 693–719). New York: Macmillan.

Moretti, E. (2013). Real wage inequality. *American Economic Journal: Applied Economics*, 5(1), 65–103.

Oliver, R. (2013). The role of ICT in higher education for the 21st century: ICT as a change agent for education. Retrieved from http://bhs-ict.pbworks.com/f/role%20of%20ict.pdf.

2 Literature review

Higher education plays a pivotal role in the economic and social growth of a country. Education increases the productive skills of individuals and also their earning power. It enables students to absorb new ideas, increase social interaction, gain access to improved health and many more tangible and intangible benefits (Kozma, 2005). Various studies have been carried out on the adoption of latest technology in higher education and its impact on economic development and human capital. Some of the relevant studies are discussed in this chapter.

NET and education

A study by Oliver (2000) found that newer technologies are able to provide strong support for teaching techniques as digital technologies provide world-class settings for competency and performance-based curricula that make sound use of these technologies. Another study by Young (2002) concludes that ICT has helped students' capability to undertake education anywhere and anytime. This flexibility has heightened the availability of just-in-time learning and provides learning opportunities for many more learners who previously were constrained by other commitments. Young also found that teachers appreciate mobile technologies and seamless communications and are able to use these technologies for supporting 24 × 7 teaching and learning.

Deaney et al. (2003) found three major reasons for using NET, i.e. the need for wider skills for effective use of tools, the need to focus on the power of technology and the need to shift familiar patterns of classroom interaction by these technologies. On the other hand, work-based learning is becoming popular with the integration of digital technologies in higher education. The authors advocate need-based learning and training, which is convenient and cost effective as it does not require travel (UNESCO, 2002). In order to face issues brought about by diversification, internationalization and marketization of higher education, it is necessary to innovatively integrate NET into higher education (Hattangdi & Ghosh, 2008). The authors argue that this will ensure good quality, accessible and affordable higher education to people in developing countries.

The use of digital technologies in tertiary education allows creation of digital resources such as digital libraries where the students, teachers and professionals can access material pertaining to their research and course work from any place at any time. These facilities allow academics to network with other researchers, helping to avoid duplication of work and ensure speedy dissemination of information to target groups (UNESCO, 2002; Chandra & Patkar, 2007). The adoption of NET provides a new teaching environment that helps to develop higher-order skills for solving complex real-world problems. It changes the characteristics of problems and tasks by enhancing the generic cognitive skills of the students as increasing volumes of information and variety of sources are easily accessible to them (Kozma, 2005).

Previous research (Budin, 1999; Johnson et al., 2012 etc.) has highlighted another aspect of technology that is related to anxiety of adoption among faculty members of Higher Education Institutions (HEIs). This primarily arises from the design and teaching of online courses but could be extended to include technology in general. This technology anxiety may occur when faculty are asked to experiment with new technologies. The faculty often lacks self-confidence when it comes to using these technologies and, as a result, they tend to avoid or resist it altogether.

NET worldwide

In a meaning-centred education framework, it is found that the use of new technologies opens up new ways of learning due to the intensive relationship between text creator and text reader (Hunt, 2013). New technology in education has two forms. First, in-house use (standalone and local area network systems) and, second, accessing classes from a remote location by using networked technologies. The second form of the technological system enables democratization of education. This aspect has been deeply analysed and discussed by Blessinger (2015). The author concluded that democratization of education leads to a reduction in educational inequality. Empirical evidence from other countries also shows that NET use is beneficial to the students. For instance, Rana and Khandaker (2015), in their study on 416 students in public and private universities in Bangladesh, revealed that availability of NET is tilted towards public universities. The authors also found that the majority of students used digital technologies for accessing information through search engines such as Google and social networking sites such as Facebook. They mainly used the Internet for downloading e-mails. Johnson et al. (2012), in their study on 25 faculty members of Carroll University, Waukesha, USA during 2010–2011, found that online faculty development programmes successfully helped them in their teaching and learning.

Basri et al. (2018) studied four Saudi Arabian Universities, two of which, namely, King Abdulaziz University and Damam University, have fully adopted technologies in the educational process, while the other two, i.e. Northern Border University and Baha University, were in the process of adopting NET in their system. The study included 1000 respondents. The findings revealed that adoption of the latest technology in the universities performs a role that is more than just academic as the students not only use this technology for searching for information on the Internet for their regular course but also use it for communication and social connections with friends and relatives. Thus these technologies are a major boost in the academic performance of students in the adopting universities as they can use it to facilitate discussions and feedback on academic matters from teachers, seniors and classmates. These kinds of interactions are necessary to improve the students' study and research skills. Another revelation of this study is that students who score higher grades are more interested in NET than their colleagues who score lower grades. This is probably because NET demands some basic knowledge in order for a student to embrace it and therefore brighter students are more likely to make use of it.

A study by Makura (2014) on 50 students' perception on NET use in a South African University argued that the adoption of digital technologies by the university has benefitted the students. Some of the advantages are improvement in memory retention, increase in motivation, understanding of concepts, promotion of collaborative learning and ease in problem-solving activities. However, students opined that university lecturers should use more ICT for teaching and learning purposes. The author further suggests that the university should sustain their e-learning programmes and training by channelling financial support if student academic performance and quality of teaching are to be enhanced. Another study by Jaffer et al. (2007) based at the University of Cape Town argues that teaching and learning may be enhanced with the use of educational technology that is driven by educational needs.

Usluel et al. (2008), in their online study of 834 faculty members of 22 Turkish universities using a structural equation model, argued that the use of ICT is getting more widespread in higher education in the country and the faculty members make use of ICT mostly as a means of communication and for carrying out research about the course through the Internet and very little for publishing their lecture notes and reading the announcements concerning the course (assignments, projects). They further conclude that ICT usage in classrooms should be more widespread, and faculty members should be supported both technically and educationally, and the process should be institutionalized by Turkish universities via a framework of policies and strategies.

Another study by Gorra and Bhati (2016) investigated the consequences of the use of digital technologies in classroom activities of 221 students from different state colleges and universities in the Caraga region of Philippines. They found that students used digital technologies for enquiring about assignments, sending and receiving e-mails, and downloading files through the Internet. The authors concluded that ICT use helped to enhance learning-related activities. One of the contributions of new technology is to make the concepts of existing theories very clear, particularly in science and engineering education. Once a concept is clear, the students can think beyond the existing knowledge and in the process new knowledge may be constructed. Hence, it is argued that NET not only helps in the dissemination of knowledge but also in the construction of knowledge.

The use of NET is useful to learners as well as society in general by means of democratization of education. This aspect augments the domain of learners. In this process, in one way or the other, society is benefitted by quality education. The concept of expanded boundaries (democratization) has been discussed in great detail by Blessinger and Cozza (2016). The contributors in the book bring out the various modes of collaboration and also highlight the potential benefits to the learners by partnering with different institutions. Tertiary education in developing countries is serving as a repository of knowledge and human capital that is expected to contribute to economic development (Lal & Paul, 2013).

Education and skill development

Quality education along with commensurate skill acts as a key enabler for inclusive growth and sustainable development. Significant progress in improving access to primary and secondary education minimizes gaps in learning outcomes. Adequate infrastructure and teacher availability can work as a catalyst in achieving the target. It is essential to integrate the use of technology in education and establish robust Educational Management Information systems to improve quality, efficiency and transparency in service delivery.

Several studies (Glaeser & Maré, 2001; Wheeler, 2001; Lal, 2005; Lal & Paul, 2015) provide evidence that the urban wage premium increases with education, suggesting that productivity effects are strongest for highly skilled workers. Another study by Morretti (2004) also shows education influences skill intensity. Data on industry and college education rates shows that productivity is increasing in the share of city workforce that is college educated. Dukić et al. (2012) studied 818 students enrolled in six Croatian polytechnics. The results indicate that ICT evolution and implementation are forcing universities and colleges to respond to trends that are capable of transforming society into a knowledge economy. The authors found that students enrolled in technical studies used ICT more intensively and the main purpose of accessing digital technologies is for using advanced mathematical packages, communication with other students and teachers, reading digital contents, etc.

Paul (2014) in his study argues that learning by doing is a new mantra for vocational education and skill development. The author concludes that smartphones and tablets have proved their multiplier effect in education and the training sector and have proved to be a success. This technology, along with existing infrastructure, could empower the current generation with job-ready skills. The use of technology can lead to low cost, high output and reduce the burden on physical infrastructure. In his study, Morretti (2004) found that a knowledgeable workforce is essential for economic productivity and concludes that skill attainment is the ultimate goal of acquiring higher education. The study also concludes that educated human resources help in increasing the productivity of a country.

Onsomu et al. (2010) used panel data from 84 countries to find that to be competitive in the technologically advanced world it is necessary to institutionalize high-level technical skill development and on-the-job training programmes at the firm level to improve upon the skills of employees. The study recommends increased participation in secondary education, technically oriented courses in tertiary education and programmes that encourage skills transfer from foreign companies.

Human capital and economic development

Economic development in developing countries in general and in India particularly depends largely on Foreign Direct Investment (FDI). According to Kemeny (2010), the transformation of FDI into technological gains depends on an economy's social capability that is measured in terms of human resource. Other studies by Alfaro et al. (2004), Borensztein et al. (1998) and Xu (2000) conclude that FDI stimulates productivity growth only when countries have reached a certain threshold of social capability. Kucera and Sarna (2004) provides robust statistical evidence that an educated workforce positively influences export performance. An article by

Globerman and Shapiro (2002) discusses the empirical evidence of human capital influencing FDI inflows. The authors found that governance infrastructure is an important determinant of FDI inflows. Another study by Lall (2000) found that R&D activity plays a significant role in attracting FDI inflows in Latin American and Asian economies.

Economic development can also be achieved through better export performance. Lal and Paul (2013) found that firms that employed highly skilled workers performed better compared to others. Export-oriented firms largely survive due to the innovation and creativity that is effectively managed by their best workforce. Hence human resources are the most vital factor for firms' innovative activity. A study by Swart and Kinnie (2003) suggests that the concept of knowledge-intensive firms should be restricted to those companies that create market value through exploitation of tacit knowledge in novel circumstances via effective management of a highly qualified workforce.

Higher education in developing countries serves as a repository of knowledge and human capital that will contribute to the development of economies (Postiglione, 2009). The importance of human capital has been captured by several other studies such as (Ducatel, 1998; Siddharthan & Lal, 2004; Lal, 2005 and others). Lal's study finds that skilled human capital is needed not only in high-technology sectors such as electronics but also in low-technology sectors such as garments manufacturing. The present era of globalization is marked with the adoption of ICT-led technologies in every sphere of life. Hence it is considered important to analyse the institutions responsible for creating innovative human capital in India. Better skills can be acquired by students if they are exposed to digital technologies during their course of study.

Various studies have been carried out on the role of education in economic development and human capital. Some of the relevant studies are discussed in this section. According to Oliver and Short (1996), adoption of ICTs into classrooms and learning settings has increased efficiency in terms of flexible programme delivery. Another study by Oliver (2000) found that ICTs are able to provide strong support for teaching techniques as they provide world-class settings for competency and performance-based curricula that make sound use of these technologies. Another study by Young (2002) concludes that ICT has helped students' capability to undertake job-oriented courses using distance learning, which has contributed to them finding more rewarding work. He also found that teachers appreciate mobile technologies and seamless communications.

Tertiary education in developing countries is serving as a major skill enhancement activity that has boosted economies (Postiglione, 2009). Many studies, such as Siddharthan and Lal (2004) and Ducatel (1998), have highlighted the significance of qualified human resources. Ducatel (1998) found that qualified manpower is essential to increase the productivity of the high-technology sector.

References

Alfaro, L., Chanda, A., Kalemli-Ozcan, S., & Sayek, S. (2004). FDI and economic growth: The role of local financial markets. *Journal of International Economics*, 64(1), 89–112.

Basri, W. S., Alandejani, J. A., & Almadani, F. M. (2018). ICT adoption impact on students' academic performance: Evidence from Saudi Universities. *Education Research International*. Retrieved from https://doi.org/10.1155/2018/1240197.

Blessinger, P. (2015). Democratizing higher education: Concluding thoughts. In P. Blessinger & J. P. Anchan (Eds.), *Democratizing Higher Education: International Comparative Perspective* (pp. 214–217). New York: Routledge.

Blessinger, P. & Cozza, B. (Eds.) (2016). *University Partnerships for Academic Programs: Professional Development*. Bingley: Emerald Publishing.

Borensztein, E., De Gregorio, J., & Lee, J. W. (1998). How does foreign direct investment affect economic growth? *Journal of International Economics*, 45(1), 115–135.

Budin, H. (1999). The computer enters the classroom. *Teachers College Record*, 100(3), 656–669.

Chandra, S., & Patkar, V. (2007). ICTS: A catalyst for enriching the learning process and library services in India. *The International Information & Library Review*, 39(1), 1–11.

Deaney, R., Ruthven, K., & Hennessy, S. (2003). Pupil perspectives on the contribution of information and communication technology to teaching and learning in the secondary school. *Research Papers in Education*, 18(2), 141–165.

Ducatel, K. (1998). *Learning and Skills in the Knowledge Economy*. DRUID Working Paper No. 98–2. Aalborg University: Danish Research Unit for Industrial Dynamics (DRUID).

Dukić, D., Dukić, G., & Kozina, G. (2012). Analysis of students' ICT usage in the function of Croatian higher education development management. *Tehnički vjesnik*, 19(2), 273–280.

Glaeser, E. L., & D. C. Maré (2001). Cities and skills. *Journal of Labor Economics*, 19(2), 316–342.

Globerman, S. & Shapiro, D. (2002). Global foreign direct investment flows: The role of governance infrastructure. *World Development*, 30(11), 1899–1919.

Gorra, V. C., & Bhati, S. S. (2016). Students' perception on use of technology in the classroom at higher education institutions in Philippines. *Asian Journal of Education and e-Learning*, 4(3), 92–103. Retrieved from http://ro.uow.edu.au/cgi/viewcontent.cgi?article=1878&context=buspapers.

Hattangdi, A. & Ghosh, A. (2008). Enhancing the quality and accessibility of higher education through the use of Information and Communication Technologies. Retrieved from www.iitk.ac.in/infocell/announce/convention/papers/Strategy%20Learning-01-Ashish%20Hattangdi,%20%20Atanu%20Ghosh.pdf.

Hunt, R. A. (2013). Meaning's secret identity. In O. Kovbasyuk & P. Blessinger (Eds.), *Meaning-Centred Education: International Perspectives & Explorations in Higher Education* (pp. 125–139). New York and Abington: Routledge.

Jaffer, S., Ng'ambi, D., & Czerniewicz, L. (2007). The role of ICTs in higher education in South Africa: One strategy for addressing teaching and learning challenges. *International Journal of Education and Development using Information and Communication Technology*, 3(4), 131–142.

Johnson, T., Wisniewski, M. A., Kuhlemeyer, G., Isaacs, G., & Krzykowski, J. (2012). Technology adoption in higher education: Overcoming anxiety through faculty bootcamp. *Journal of Asynchronous Learning Networks*, 16(2), 63–72.

Kemeny, T. (2010). Does foreign direct investment drive technological upgrading? *World Development*, 38(11), 1543–1554.

Kozma, R. (2005). National policies that connect ICT-based education reform to economic and social development. *Human Technology*, 1(2), 117–156.

Kucera, D., & Sarna, R. (2004). *Child Labour, Education and Export Performance*. ILO Working Paper No. 52, 1–46. Geneva: ILO.

Lal, K. (2005). E-business, entrepreneurship, organizational restructuring: Evidence from Indian firms. In A. Saith & M. Vijayabhaskar (Eds.), *ICTs and Indian Economic Development: Economy, Work, Regulation* (pp. 366–385). New Delhi and London: Sage Publications.

Lal, K., & Paul, S. (2013). Export orientation and corporate policy during global economic slowdown. In H. Hirakawa, K. Lal, N. Shinkai, & T. Norio, (Eds.), *Servitization, IT-ization and Innovation Models: Two-stage Industrial Cluster Theory* (pp. 150–164). London and New York: Routledge.

Lal, K. & Paul, S. (2015). Quality of teachers and skill formation in students. *Indian Journal of Teacher Education*, 1(1), 85–98.

Lall, S. (2000). Export performance, technological upgrading and foreign direct investment strategies in the Asian newly industrializing economies: With special reference to Singapore. *Series Productive Development no. 88*, October, 1–69.

Makura, A. H. (2014). Students' perceptions of the use of ICT in a higher education teaching and learning context: The case of a South African University. *Mediterranean Journal of Social Sciences*, 5(11), 43–47.

Moretti, E. (2004). Workers' education, spillovers, and productivity: Evidence from plant-level production functions. *The American Economic Review*, 94(3), 656–690.

Oliver, R. (2000). Creating meaningful contexts for learning in web-based settings. *Proceedings of Open Learning 2000*, 53–62, Brisbane: Learning Network, Queensland.

Oliver, R., & Short, G. (1996). The Western Australian telecentres network: A model for enhancing access to education and training in rural areas. *International Journal of Educational Telecommunications*, 2(4), 311–328.

Onsomu, E. N., Ngware, M. W., & Manda, D. K. (2010). The impact of skills development on competitiveness: Empirical evidence from a cross-country analysis. *Educational Policy Analysis Archives*, 18(7), 1–21.

Paul, S. (2014). The impact of technology on skill development. *Indian Journal of Industrial Relations*, 49(3), 401–408.

Postiglione, G. (2009). Education impact study: The global recession and the capacity of colleges and universities to serve vulnerable populations in Asia. Retrieved from www.adbi.org/workingpaper/2010/03/29/3644.education.impact.study.

Rana, J. & Khandaker, S. (2015). Challenges of ICT in higher education: A comparison of uses and perception among students in a public and private university in Bangladesh. *Conference Proceeding of the International Conference on Innovating Education in Asia*, 31 October–2 November. New Delhi.

Siddharthan, N. S., & Lal, K. (2004). Liberalization and growth of firms in India. In C. H. H. Rao, B. B. Bhattacharya, & N. S. Siddharthan (Eds.), *Indian Economy and Society: In the Era of Globalization and Liberalization* (pp. 265–278). New Delhi: Academic Publications.

Swart, J., & Kinnie, N. (2003). Knowledge-intensive firms: The influence of the client on HR systems. *Human Resource Management Journal*, 13(3), 37–55.

UNESCO (2002). *Open and Distance Learning Trends, Policy and Strategy Considerations*. Paris: UNESCO. Retrieved from http://unesdoc.unesco.org/images/0012/001284/128463e.pdf.

Usluel, Y. K., Aşkar, P., & Baş, T. (2008). A structural equation model for ICT usage in higher education. *Educational Technology & Society*, 11 (2), 262–273.

Wheeler, C. (2001). Search, sorting, and urban agglomeration. *Journal of Labor Economics*, 19(4), 879–899.

Xu, B. (2000). Multinational enterprises, technology diffusion, and host country productivity growth. *Journal of Development Economics*, 62(2), 477–493.

Young, J. (2002). The 24-hour professor. *The Chronicle of Higher Education*, 48 (38), 31–33.

3 Profile of institutions and degree of NET use

Introduction

The year 1991 is recognized as the year of liberalization of the Indian economy. With the liberalization of economic policies, due attention was also paid to the education sector and the entry of the private sector in education was highly encouraged, resulting in many autonomous institutions converting into deemed universities and also the opening of state private universities. It is worth mentioning here that universities in India are governed and financed by either central or state governments. Universities governed by central government are called central universities while universities governed by states are known as state universities.

In the era of liberalization of Indian education, the private sector was encouraged by the government to establish new higher education institutions. The private HEIs permitted by states are called private state universities. Such institutions do not receive any financial support from the state. Private sector universities also need to comply with the University Grants Commission (UGC), India under the UGC Act 2003 (Establishment of and Maintenance of Standards in Private Universities Regulation) in order to create a standard uniform education across the country. Over the past three decades, 340 private universities have been established in the private sector (www.ugc.ac.in/privatuniversity.aspx). A scenario of HEIs in India is presented in Appendix I. The data for Appendix I is taken from the Ministry of Human Resource Development, Government of India.

Although the use of information technology (IT) in governance was encouraged by the Government of India in the mid-1980s; education institutions were provided financial and other support to use digital technologies in HEIs in the early 1990s. The state governments followed this also. Consequently, central and state-funded universities adopted limited use of IT. The complexity of technology and inadequate resources constrained the use of IT in these institutions. With the advent of the Internet in the mid-1990s in India, the use of digital technologies percolated down to many other activities. The adoption did not get the desired momentum due to the archaic procurement procedures followed in government institutions. After the private universities came into existence, the adoption and use of IT gained momentum. This was primarily due to two reasons. First, the availability of function-specific ICT tools and, second, the competition among private universities.

Although the Ministry of Human Resource Development conducts an annual survey of HEIs known as the All India Survey of Higher Education (AISHE), it collects limited information on knowledge infrastructure. To date, the availability and use of digital technologies in HEIs is an under-researched area in India. This study, perhaps the first one based on a primary survey, has made an attempt to ascertain the causes and consequences of use of new technologies in HEIs. Since the education sector in India consists of central, state and private universities, this study covers all three types of institution in order to produce the most reliable and robust findings.

India is a vast country with huge ethnic, social and cultural variations. It would have been better to include some institutions located in other parts of the country. This was not possible due to financial constraints. However, it is believed that the intensity of adoption and use of ICTs may be invariant across the regions of the country as the standard of higher education is controlled by UGC.

This chapter presents a profile of institutions and data analysis of students. The statistical analysis includes univariate, bivariate and multivariate. The multivariate techniques encompass Cluster and Discriminant analysis. The data were collected from seven HEIs located in National Capital Region (NCR), India. The institutions are: University of Delhi, Delhi; Jawaharlal Nehru University, Delhi; Jamia Millia Islamia University, Delhi; Gautam Buddha University, Greater New Okhla Industrial Development Authority (GNOIDA); Northcap University, Gurgaon; Ansal University, Gurgaon; and Symbiosis International University, NOIDA. The survey of these universities was conducted during July 2015 to October 2016. The sample consists of 201 students and 43 faculty members. The data were collected using a semi-structured questionnaire. The questionnaires for students, teachers and management are presented in Appendix III, IV and V respectively.

Profile of institutions

The study includes representative sample of universities located in the NCR. Due care has been taken to include public and private-funded institutions. Their profiles are presented in this subsection.

Jawaharlal Nehru University

Jawaharlal Nehru University (JNU) is a central university established by The Jawaharlal Nehru University Act 1966 on 22 April 1969. The university has a huge campus of 1019.38 acres in the South of Delhi. The university has 37 centres offering traditional to modern courses such as computer science. It offers undergraduate, postgraduate and research programmes in sciences, social sciences, environment and international studies. More than 7000 students were enrolled in the university during 2014–2015.

It is very costly to make the entire campus Wi-Fi enabled due to its sprawling nature. However several schools and centres are equipped with the latest communication and networking technologies. The university claims that, in addition to a central computer server, departmental servers have also been installed. The university management claimed that they have access to cloud computing technologies as well which might be used for teaching in IT and computer science-related courses. As far as NET usage is concerned, it is heavily used for administrative activities such as student admissions, fee collection, preparation of results, and maintaining e-records of teachers, students and employees. As far as the usage of NET in academic activities is concerned, it is used for accessing library resources and also students used the new technologies for preparing project reports. It was stated that faculty preferred offline teaching in the classroom.

Jamia Millia Islamia

Established in 1920 at Aligarh, Jamia Millia Islamia (JMI) became a central university located in Delhi in 1988. Spread over 215.85 acres in South Delhi, JMI had 14,636 students enrolled in 2011–2012. The university offers undergraduate, postgraduate and research programme in sciences, social sciences, commerce, engineering, law and management. The Wi-Fi is functional in several departments individually. In addition to central computing facilities, it provides computational facilities in some departments. Like other universities, cloud computing technology is limited to teaching and learning purposes.

The level of use of digital technologies is similar to that of other public-funded universities. The managerial functions such as financial management, student admission and fee collection, preparation of results and maintenance of e-records are performed using new technologies. Within the academic applications of new technologies, the university has a digital library and syllabus and reading material is made available online. The classrooms are equipped with online facilities in engineering courses only. The faculty uses standalone systems in most of the courses but online also in few. The students prefer the use of standalone devices in preparing assignments and projects.

University of Delhi

Established in 1922, the University of Delhi is recognized as one of the premier academic institutions in India. The university started with three colleges and 750 students. Within a span of almost a century, it has 16 faculties, over 80 academic departments and around 90 colleges. The university has over seven lakh students and offers 500 programmes. With the expansion of the university, the government decided to set up another campus for better management and coordination of academic and administrative activities. Consequently, the South Campus was established in 1973 and moved to its present location on Benito Juarez Road, near Dhaula Kuan, in 1984, which is spread across 69 acres of green land. The university offers degrees in sciences, arts, commerce, law, medicine, engineering etc. The PhD programmes offered by the university are well recognized worldwide.

As far as the ICT infrastructure is concerned, the university has been installing up-to-date technology. The university was one of the few institutions in India that had computer systems in the 1960s. Subsequently, it acquired IBM 360 during the 1970s. With the advent of Internet and e-mail, the university embarked on setting up a campus area network. However, in the initial days, due to the complexity of network technologies, many schools and departments acquired their own individual networks. As of now, the university has laid a fibre-optic network in the North and the South Campuses, connecting all colleges and departments.

Gautam Buddha University

Gautam Buddha University (GBU) is a state university of Uttar Pradesh established by the Uttar Pradesh Gautam Buddha University Act 2002. Located in Greater NOIDA and established in 2002, the campus is spread over 511 acres. The number of students enrolled in 2014–2015 was 3200. The university offers undergraduate and postgraduate courses in traditional streams such as BA, BSc and BCom. It specializes in engineering and management education. It offers undergraduate and postgraduate courses in these disciplines. In addition, the university has PhD programme in certain subjects.

Despite being a vast campus, the university has been able to make the entire site Wi-Fi enabled. This might have been possible due to huge one-time grant provided to the university. The funding came from the government of Uttar Pradesh, NOIDA and Greater NOIDA authorities. As far as the computing facilities are concerned, they have set up a central server to cater to the computing needs of the university. The institution did not have a cloud computing facility in the campus. Being a relatively new institution, the usage of digital technologies in managerial functions is limited. The financial management of the university is partially digital. New technologies are being used for the admission of students and preparation of results only. Among academic activities, the institution has online library resources and syllabus and reading material is also made available online. The institution has not been able to provide class notes online. Although classrooms are equipped with standalone and online facilities, the students prefer to work on standalone systems.

Northcap University

Northcap University (NCU) a private university. Prior to becoming a university in 2009 it was a technical training institution (Institute of Technology and Management) established in 1996 and was affiliated to Maharshi Dayanand University, Rohtak. In 2015 it changed its name to Northcap University. Located in Gurgaon now Guru Gram, Haryana in the NCR, the university offers science, technology, law and management courses. Along with graduate and postgraduate courses, it offers PhD programmes in limited disciplines. More than 3000 students were enrolled in the university in 2014–2015. Having a very compact and integrated building, the university provides Wi-Fi facilities over the entire campus of ten acres. In addition to centralized computing facilities, it also provides departmental facilities. The cloud computing facility is limited to teaching and learning to engineering students.

As far as NET usage is concerned, it is highly used in managerial as well as academic functions. In addition to usual tasks such as financial management, online admission and fee collection, preparation of results, e-records of students, teachers and employees, it provides facilities for student login and evaluation of faculty by students. The performance of teachers is evaluated by students through their individual logins and passwords. The university has a well-equipped e-library with online access to several journals such as those affiliated to the Institute of Electrical and Electronics Engineers (IEEE), Association for Computing Machinery (ACM) etc. The university has developed an e-learning management system (LMS) through which students can access online syllabus and course contents. Online class notes are available on the system for selected courses. The classrooms are equipped with online teaching systems. The students are found to be using standalone as well as online systems. The university has installed a plagiarism check software called Turnitin on a standalone system, which is used for research checking output by faculty and students.

Ansal University

Ansal University is also a private university. Prior to becoming a university in 2012, it was a technical training institute (Ansal Institute of Technology) established in 2000 and was affiliated to Guru Govind Singh Indraprastha University. The university is located in Gurgaon (now Guru Gram), Haryana. In addition to design and architectural courses, which have been main focus of the university, it offers undergraduate and postgraduate courses in sciences, social sciences, engineering and management. PhD programmes are also available in limited subjects. There were 812 students enrolled in 2014–2015.

Being a compact campus, the university has been able to make the entire campus Wi-Fi enabled. Like other universities, they have also provided computing facilities at the department level. Cloud computing is available for training purposes. As far as the usage of NET is concerned, it is heavily used for administrative functions such as financial management (fee, receipt, salary slips, biometrics, etc.), online admission, preparation of results, e-records (students, teachers and staff) and evaluation of faculty by students. The university has good e-library resources. The detailed syllabus and reading material is available on the university website. The institution is in the process of making class notes available online. The new technologies are being effectively used by faculty and students. The classrooms are equipped with standalone and online facilities for certain courses. It was reported that NET are heavily used in engineering and information technology-related courses followed by management and research programmes. The use of NET was found to be limited in traditional courses such as Law, BA, BCom, BSc, MA, MCom and MSc.

Symbiosis International University

Established in 2002, Symbiosis International University (SIU) is located at the Symbiosis Knowledge Village on the outskirts of Pune on a 300-acre campus. Accreditation of repeatedly grade 'A' by the National Assessment and Accreditation Council (NAAC) speaks to the academic standard maintained by the university. SIU has established need-based institutions across the eight faculties of law, management, computer studies, health and biomedical, media, communication and design, engineering, and humanities and social sciences. Although Symbiosis has been in management education since 1978, it established the Symbiosis Centre for Management Education in Pune in 2004 and extended its arm in NCR in 2010 by setting up a centre in NOIDA. Keeping in mind the scope of the study, the survey includes the centre located in NOIDA, which has two faculties, i.e. law and management.

The Symbiosis Centre for Management Studies (SCMS) NOIDA had 450 students in 2014–2015. Not a single seat goes vacant in the institute. In fact students are admitted through a written test followed by interview. The institute receives four to five times more applications than the seats available. SCMS has been successfully able to maintain its academic standard by providing up-to-date digital infrastructure and the best possible faculty. The entire campus is Wi-Fi enabled. As far as the use of digital technologies in managerial functions is concerned, it is used in almost all the functions. These include financial management, online admission and fee payment, preparation of results, maintenance of students and teachers' records. Every student is provided with an individual login and password for interaction with SCMS. Online evaluation of faculty by the students is carried out on an annual basis, which helps faculty in improving the teaching standards. SCMS is one of the few self-financed institutions that provide provision of verification of degrees/certificates issued by the centre.

NET use and students

For univariate and bivariate analysis, only figures are presented in this subsection while the details of the data are presented in Appendix 3.1.

Univariate analysis

Apart from personal information, details of NET used by the students and the impact on them were collected. The information on impediments of using NET was also gathered. With regard to gender distribution of students, 64.2 per cent are males while 35.8 per cent are females. The majority (38.8 per cent) of students fall in the age group of 21–23 years while 37.3 and 23.9 per cent belong to the age group of 18–20 and 24+ years respectively. The distribution of students by the course they were pursuing is presented in Figure 3.1.

As far as distribution of students by their study stream is concerned, 27.9 per cent belong to engineering and 23.4 per cent are research scholars (MPhil or PhD). The percentage of students pursuing management courses is 25.4 per cent while 16.4 and 5.5 percentage belong to science and arts

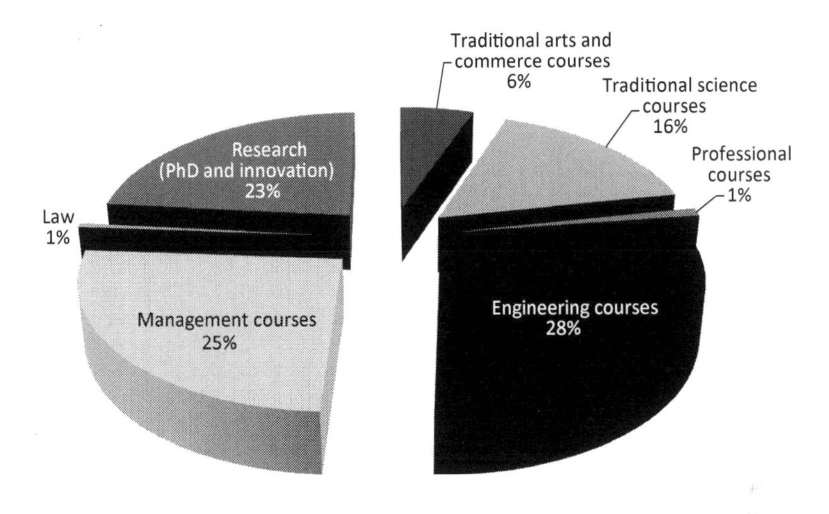

Figure 3.1 Distribution of students by the course.

and commerce stream respectively. Merely 1.0 and 0.5 per cent are pursuing professional courses and law respectively. The professional courses include media and nursing. It can be seen from Figure 3.1 that the highest percentage is of engineering students. This is because all the sample students from Ansal and Northcap universities were pursuing engineering courses and also many of the students from JNU were pursuing courses in computer science. The majority of the students (98.5 per cent) are studying on a full-time basis.

The information on access to NET (personal and institutional) was also collected. Their responses are presented in Figure 3.2.

Figure 3.2 indicates that a very high percentage (65.2 per cent) had their own laptop with Internet facility. It can also be seen from Figure 3.2 that 24.9 per cent had access to a desktop with Internet in their homes. A fairly good percentage of respondents, 10.4 and 8.0 per cent, owned tablets and e-readers respectively. As far as the provision of NET by institutions is concerned, the highest percentage (76.6 per cent) reported that desktop with Internet was made available by their institution. This is quite obvious because the institutional labs are equipped with desktop with Internet. It was found during the survey that students studying in postgraduate programmes (engineering and management) were also provided laptops with Internet. The percentage of students who shared this view is 19.9 per cent. Figure 3.2 also indicates that standalone laptops are no longer a preferred choice, which is quite obvious as the Internet is now an integral part of laptops. The provision of tablets and e-readers are not a viable option for institutions.

Information regarding use of various components of NET was collected from the students. Their responses are presented in Figure 3.3.

Figure 3.3 indicates that 84.1 per cent of the respondents opined that intranet is available in their institution while 86.6 per cent reported that their campus is Wi-Fi enabled. The majority (41.8 per cent) reported

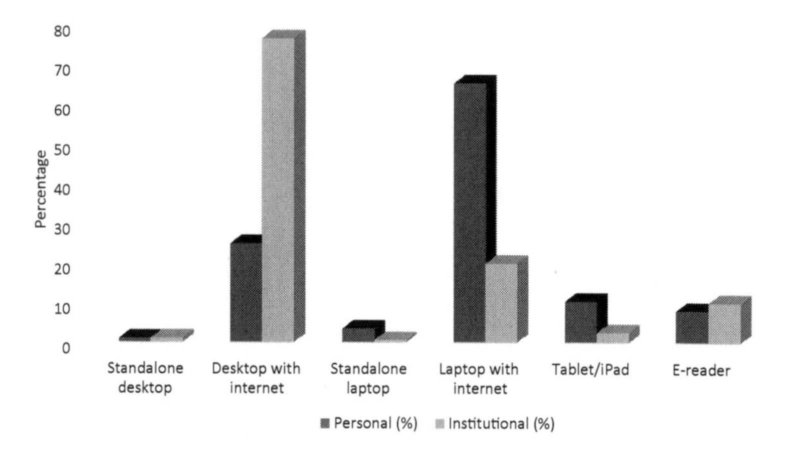

Figure 3.2 Accessibility of NET.

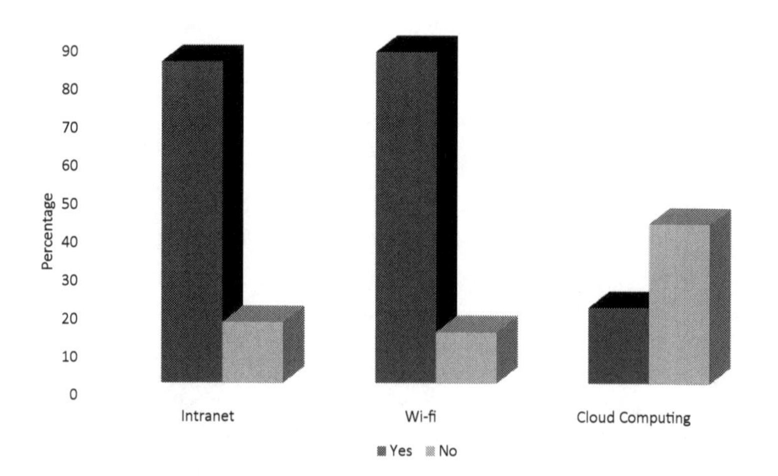

Figure 3.3 Accessibility of network technologies.

that the cloud computing facility is not available in the institution. A small percentage (19.9 per cent) claimed that the facility is available. All the respondents who reported availability of cloud computing belonged to the engineering faculty and cloud computing may be part of their course curriculum. As far as the speed of Internet provided by the institution is concerned, the majority (55.7 per cent) of respondents opined that it is <100 MBPS while 31.8 per cent respondents indicated the speed to be between 100 MBPS and <1 GBPS. A small percentage of respondents (6.5 per cent) claimed the speed of Internet in their institution is >1 GBPS.

The next query pertains to the degree of NET use. The responses were collected on a 3-point scale i.e. 1 'limited users', 2 'moderate users', 3 'extensive users'. The limited users are those who use e-mails and Internet while moderate users are those who use e-mail and Internet along with limited online class activities. The extensive NET users are those who use digital technologies for all of their needs such as e-mail, Internet, online class activities etc. The distribution of students by the extent of NET use is reported in Figure 3.4.

Figure 3.4 shows that around 40 per cent (40.8 per cent) of respondents used NET to a limited extent while just 21.9 per cent are found to be extensive users of the new technologies. The percentage of moderate users of NET is 37.3 per cent.

Figure 3.5 presents the analysis of purpose of NET use. The various purposes can be grouped into two categories, namely: academic and managerial.

It can be seen from Figure 3.5 that among the academic activities, 71.1 per cent responded that they use digital technologies for downloading

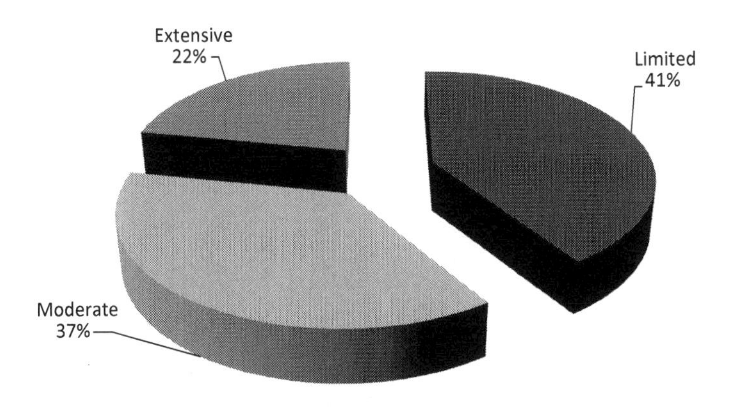

Figure 3.4 Extent of use of NET.

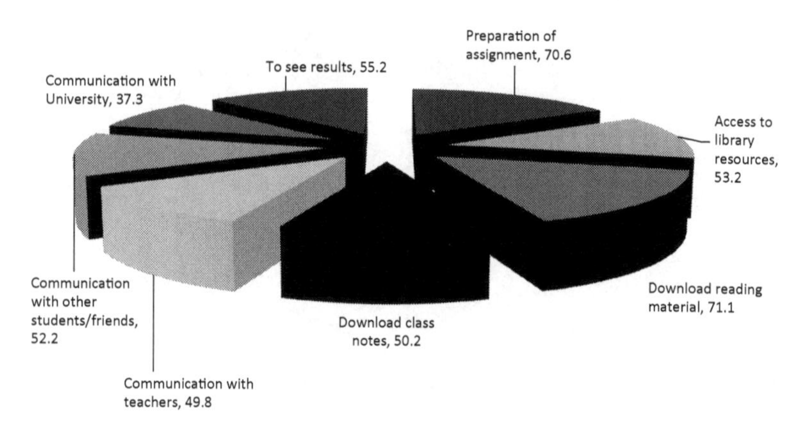

Figure 3.5 Purpose of use of NET (percentage).

reading material. This is followed by preparation of assignments where the response rate is 70.6 per cent. Roughly 55 (55.2) per cent used NET to see results. On the other hand just 37.3 per cent opined that they were using digital technologies for communicating with university.

The opinion on relevance of digital technologies in various activities was sought from the students. The opinions were collected on a 4-point scale, i.e. 1 'Not useful', 2 'Neutral', 3 'Useful' and 4 'Very useful'. The average scores are presented in Figure 3.6.

It can be seen from Figure 3.6 that the utility of NET in understanding concepts more clearly has been assigned the highest score, i.e. 3.15, suggesting that a substantially large percentage of students found digital technologies to be very relevant. This is substantiated by the fact that 40.3 and 32.8 per cent of students found it useful and very useful respectively. The second most relevant aspect in the opinion of students is better illustration of ideas. The composite score of this aspect is 3.08. An almost similar score has been assigned to the convenience aspect.

The next question is on the impact of NET use on the students. The impact of new technologies was measured on a 5-point scale, namely, 1 'strongly disagree', 2 'disagree', 3 'neutral', 4 'agree', 5 'strongly agree'. The average scores are presented in Figure 3.7.

Figure 3.7 indicates that a substantially high percentage of students opined that the NET enables better communication and collaboration with classmates with the highest average score of 3.58. The percentage of students who consider it agreeable and strongly agreeable is 35.3 and 14.9 respectively. The next important impact opined by the students is skill development, with

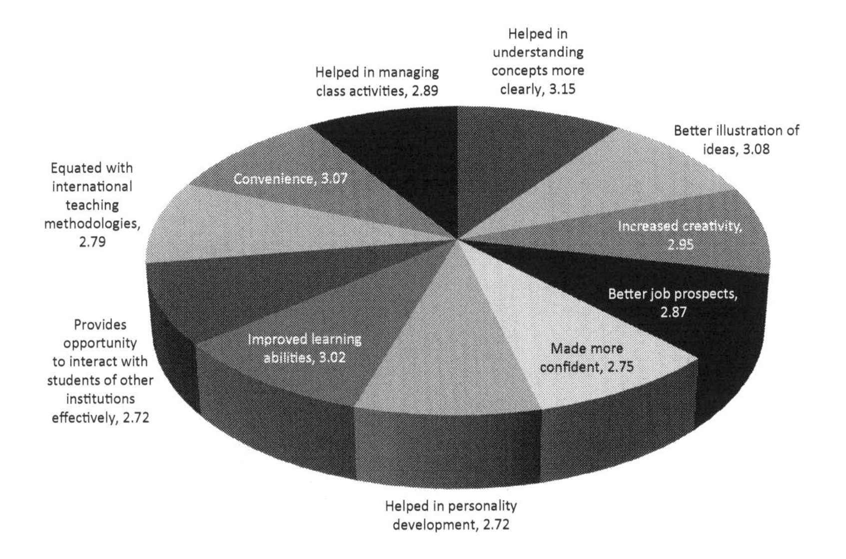

Figure 3.6 Relevance of digital technologies in various activities.

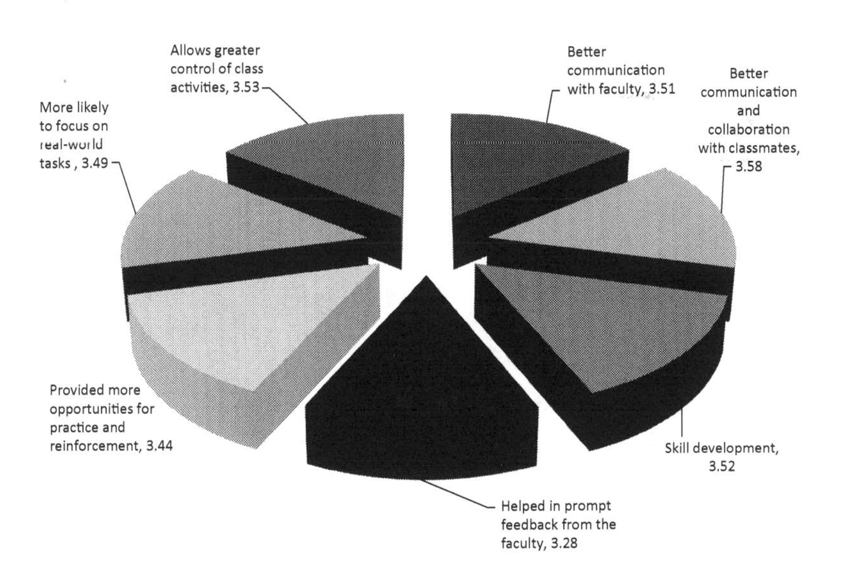

Figure 3.7 Impact of new technology use.

an average score of 3.52. It can be seen from the figure that the opinions related to skill development follow the similar pattern as that of better communication and collaboration with classmates. The third most important impact is that NET use allows greater control of class activities.

The next query pertains to the contributions of NET use in improving learning and managing class activities. The opinions were sought on 4-point scale, i.e. 1 'Did not use', 2 'Negative effect', 3 'No effect', 4 'Improved learning'. The analysis is presented in Figure 3.8.

Figure 3.8 shows that 'online sharing material among students' received the highest score of 3.41 suggesting that a substantially large percentage of students opined in favour of improved learning. The percentage of such students is 57.2. The second most important activity is 'online reading' with an average score of 3.22. An almost similar percentage (54.2) to that of most important activity considered that use of NET contributes significantly in online reading. The third most important activity in the opinion of students is 'submitting assignments online'.

The successful use of digital technologies is dependent on external as well as internal factors. The internal factors are IT setup within the institution while external factors are communication networks. In order to understand the impediments related to internal as well as external factors, the opinion of students on the barriers of NET use was sought. The opinions were measured on a 4-point scale with 1 'Not at all', 2 'To some extent', 3 'Moderate', 4 'Major barrier'. The average score of barriers of NET usage are depicted in Figure 3.9.

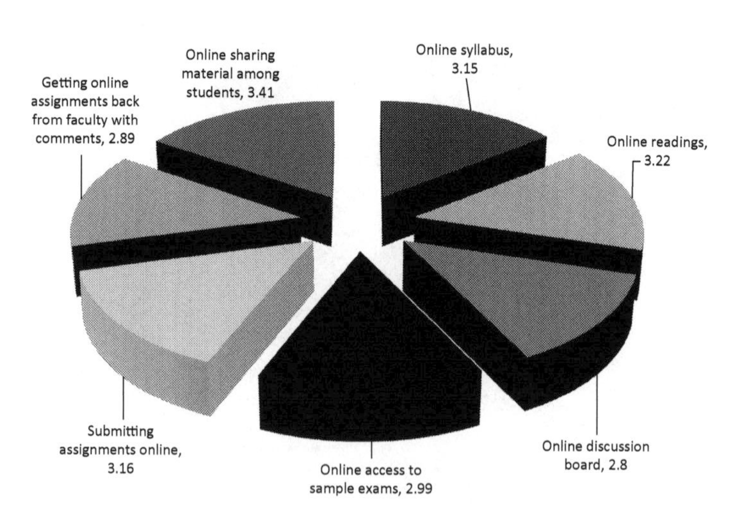

Figure 3.8 NET use and improvement in learning and managing classes.

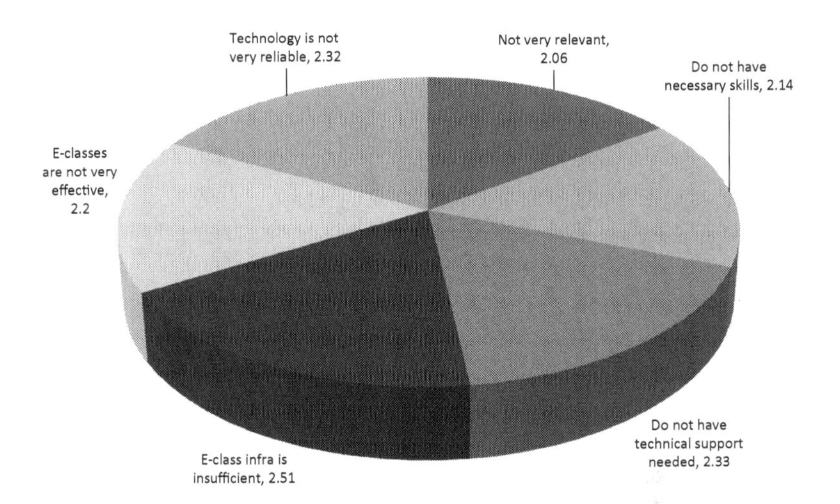

Figure 3.9 Barriers for using e-class.

Figure 3.9 indicates that the average score of all the barriers is around 2, suggesting that the students considered them as barriers to some extent. Among all the aspects, the insufficiency of e-class infrastructure is rated the highest, followed by lack of technical support and non-reliability of technology. Figure 3.9 also shows that none of these aspects are considered to be a major barrier to NET use.

Bivariate analysis

In bivariate analysis, efforts have been made to identify the association between the degree of NET use with various aspects of students. In this context, the first aspect pertains to course of study. As far as the data on degree of NET use is concerned, it was collected on a 3-point scale, namely: 'Limited use', 'Moderate use', 'Extensive use'. The association between course of study and extent on NET use is presented in Figure 3.10.

Figure 3.10 shows that that there is strong association between degree of NET use and the course being pursued by students. This is substantiated by the fact that the majority of students who were pursuing engineering courses are either moderate or extensive users of NET, while the highest percentage of limited users of NET are those who pursue either traditional science or management courses. Chi-square tests suggest that the association is significant at the highest level, i.e. 1 per cent.

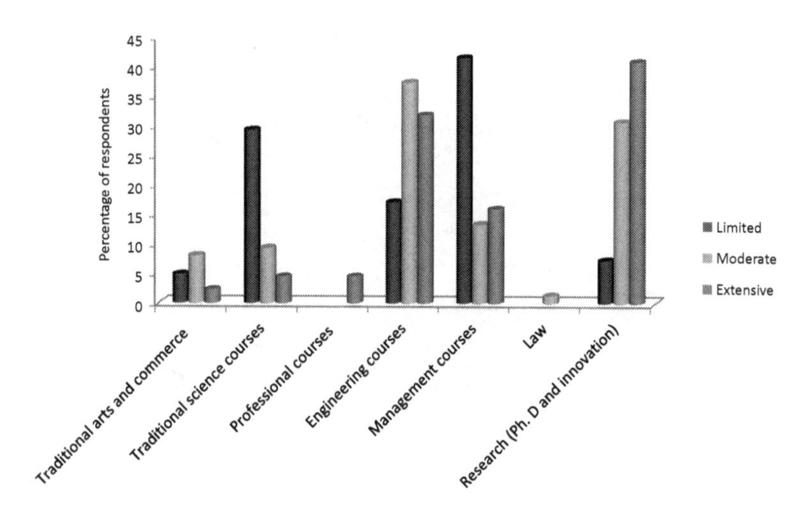

Figure 3.10 Degree of NET used and course of study.

Figure 3.11 presents the distribution of students by their age and degree of NET use. The age was measured on a 3-point scale, i.e. 1 '18–20', 2 '21–23' and 3 '24+'. The relationship seems to be an inverted U shaped in general.

It can be seen from Figure 3.11 that a substantially high percentage (56.1) of limited users of NET fall into the age group of 18–20 years while the highest percentage (47.7) of extensive users of NET belong to the age group of 24+ years. On the other hand almost 50 (46.7) per cent of moderate users belong to the age group of 21–23 years. Figure 3.11 also shows that the percentage of students (24+ years) increases with intensity of NET use while it decreases in the age group of 18–20 years. Based on the results, it may be inferred that senior students use NET more extensively. The association between intensity of NET use and age is statistically significant at the highest level.

Out of the seven institutions surveyed, four are owned by the government and three are self-financed. The distribution of students by intensity of NET use and nature of financial status is presented in Figure 3.12.

It can be seen from Figure 3.12 that the trend of NET use in both types of universities is very different. Between the limited users of NET, 68.3 per cent belong to self-financed institutions while this is reversed among extensive users as 63.6 per cent come from public-funded universities. It was expected that self-financed universities might be better equipped with the latest digital technologies as they face severe

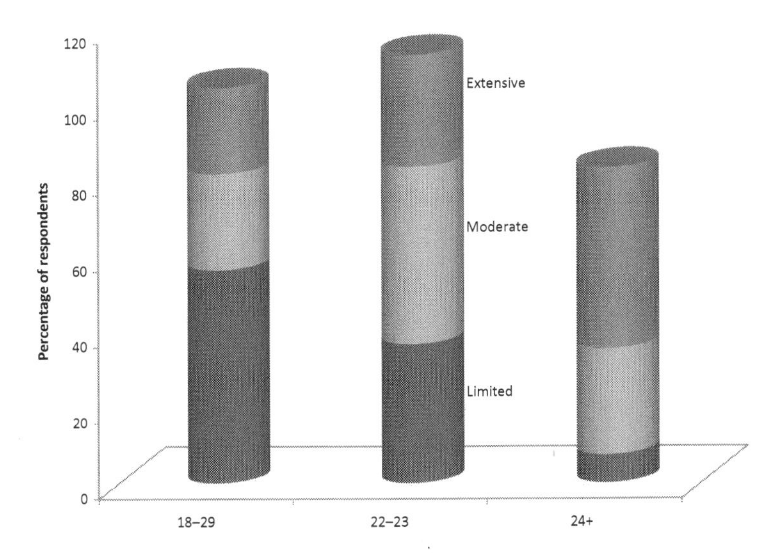

Figure 3.11 Degree of NET used and age of students.

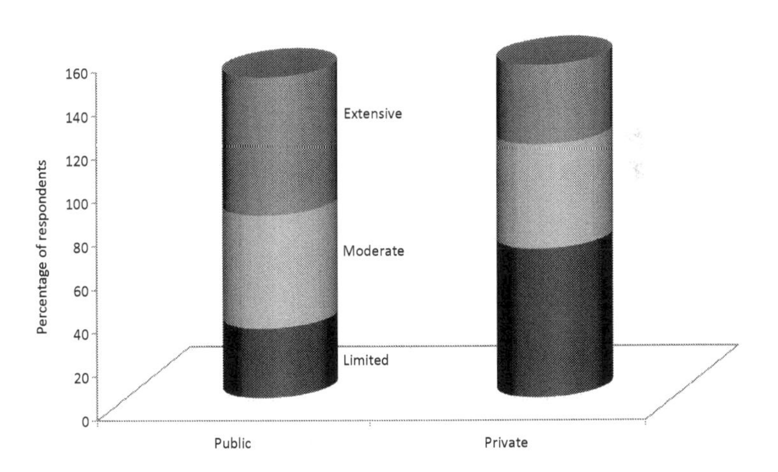

Figure 3.12 Degree of NET used and financial status of the institution.

competition in attracting students. Consequently students studying in these universities are expected to use NET more extensively. However, the findings do not support the argument. Given the pattern of NET use, the association between intensity of NET use and the financial nature of the institutions is statistically significant at the highest level of significance (1 per cent). The high percentage of extensive users of NET could be attributed to the fact that almost all the research scholars are registered at the public-funded universities and it is they who are extensive users of digital technologies.

The students were asked to give their opinion about the relevance of digital technologies to their course of study. The opinions are of several aspects of relevance such as 'Helped in understanding concepts more clearly', 'Better illustration of ideas', 'Increased creativity', 'Better job prospects', 'Makes more confident', 'Helped in personality development', 'Improves learning abilities', 'Provides opportunity to interact with students of other institutions effectively', 'Equated with international teaching methodologies', 'Convenience', 'Helped in managing class activities (e.g. planning, apportioning time etc.)'. The bivariate analysis focuses on three most important aspects. They are 'helped in understanding concepts more clearly' (relevance-1), 'better illustration of ideas' (relevance-2), and 'convenience' (relevance-3). The analysis of relevance-1 is presented in Figure 3.13.

Figure 3.13 shows that the largest percentage of NET users opined that it is either useful or very useful for them. Among the category of limited users, 34.1 per cent of students opined that use of NET is useful while 26.8 per cent viewed NET use as very useful. On the other hand, in the category of moderate and extensive users of NET, the scenario is almost similar. Figure 3.13 also shows that around 5 per cent of students felt that NET use is not useful for their course. Such respondents may belong to the social sciences stream. Statistically the association between intensity of NET use and relevance-1 is significant at the 10 per cent level.

The second most important aspect is that NET use helps in better illustration of ideas. The association between degree of NET use and this aspect is presented in Figure 3.14.

Figure 3.14 indicates that an almost similar opinion to that of relevance-1 has been expressed by the students. The highest percentage (45.5) of students in the extensive NET usage category opined that it is very useful for their course. Among the moderate users, 38.7 per cent considered NET use as useful. A noticeable fact is that none of the extensive users viewed NET use as not useful. The findings also suggest that association between degree of NET use and relevance-2 is statistically significant at the 10 per cent level.

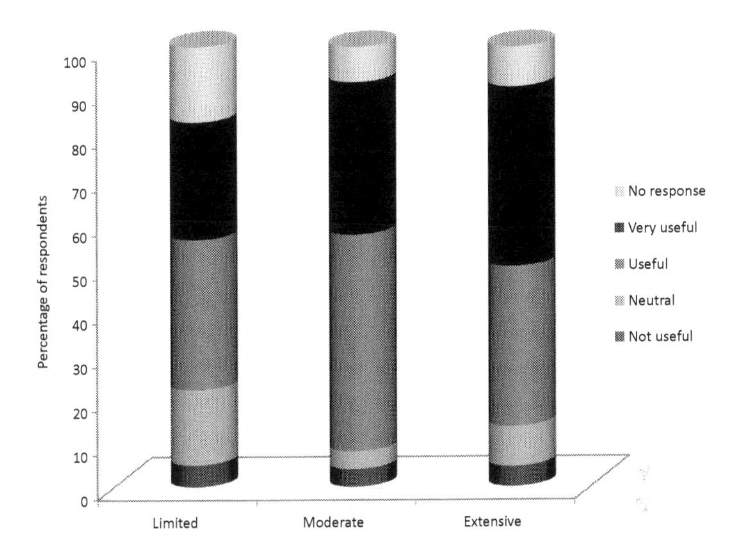

Figure 3.13 Degree of NET used and its relevance-1.

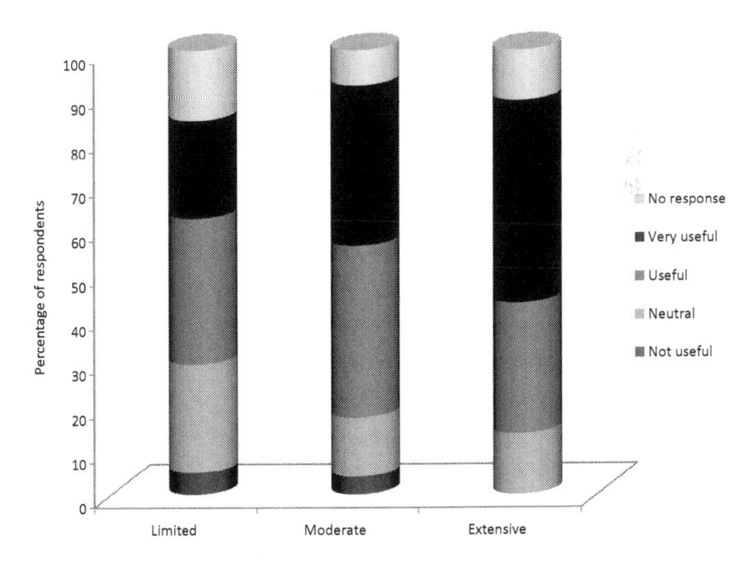

Figure 3.14 Degree of NET used and its relevance-2.

Figure 3.15 presents the analysis of third most important relevance and the intensity of NET use. It can be seen from the figure that the scenario is similar to that of the other two aspects. The percentage of students of moderate and extensive users who viewed NET use as very useful is higher than relevance-2. The percentage is 48.5 and 56.8 respectively in moderate and extensive users. Another noticeable fact is that the percentage of students who are neutral to this aspect is higher than both the other two aspects. The association is statistically more robust and significant at the 5 per cent level.

The opinion of the students on the impact of new technologies on them was also sought. The opinion was collected on many aspects. However the bivariate analysis focuses on the three most important impacts of NET use. As can be seen in univariate analyses of impacts, the most important impact is that NET use provides opportunities to better communicate and collaborate with classmates. The analysis of this aspect is presented in Figure 3.16.

It can be seen from Figure 3.16 that more than half of the students (55.5 per cent) agreed or strongly agreed that NET use has a positive impact on them as far as ease of communication with other students is concerned. A very small percentage (11.0 per cent) disagreed or strongly disagreed on this aspect. Roughly one-third did not express any opinion. Figure 3.16 also shows that 58.9 per cent of extensive users either agreed or strongly

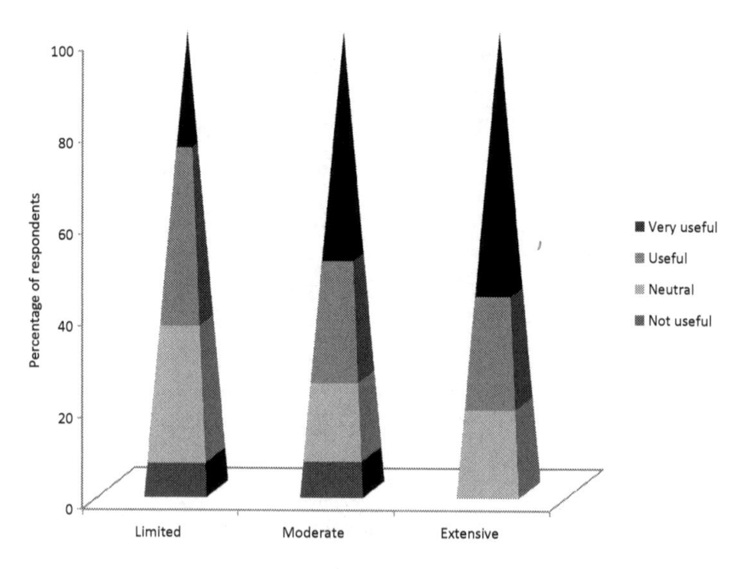

Figure 3.15 Degree of NET used and its relevance-3.

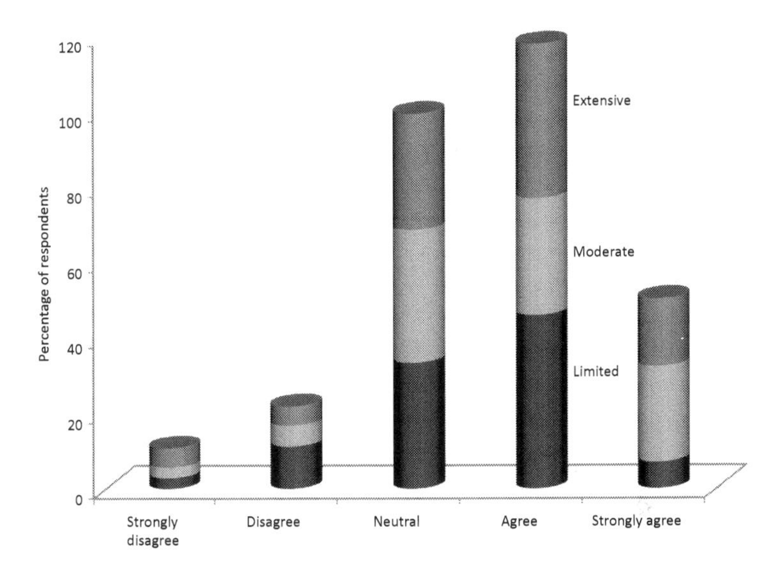

Figure 3.16 Degree of NET used and its impact-1.

agreed that there is a positive impact of NET use in better communicating with classmates. The figure also shows that the pattern of opinion related to 'agree' or 'strongly agree' in all categories of NET use is similar. However, the association between the degree of NET use and impact-1 is insignificant. It signifies that irrespective of intensity of degree of NET use, the majority of students are in favour of agree or strongly agree. The degree of NET use does not influence their opinion.

As identified in univariate analysis the second most important impact is skill development. The association between the degree of NET use and this impact is presented in Figure 3.17.

It can be seen from Figure 3.17 that the pattern of opinion on this aspect is similar to that of first impact. The highest percentage in all the categories of NET users belongs to students who agreed that NET use helps them in skill development, while the percentage of students who strongly agreed with this is around 10 per cent in all the categories. It seems the opinion of students is not influenced by the degree of NET use. This is captured by Chi-squared test that suggests that Chi-sq value is insignificant.

The third most important impact of NET use is that it allows greater control of class activities. The analysis of this impact is presented in Figure 3.18.

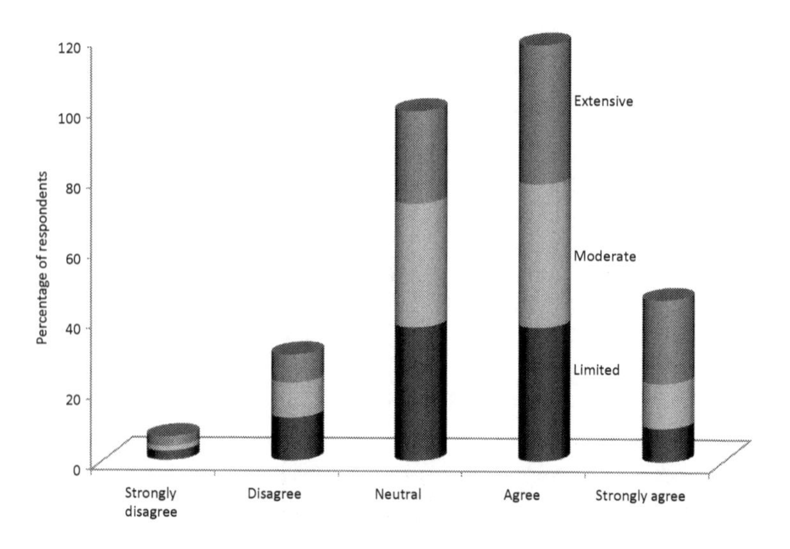

Figure 3.17 Degree of NET used and its impact-2.

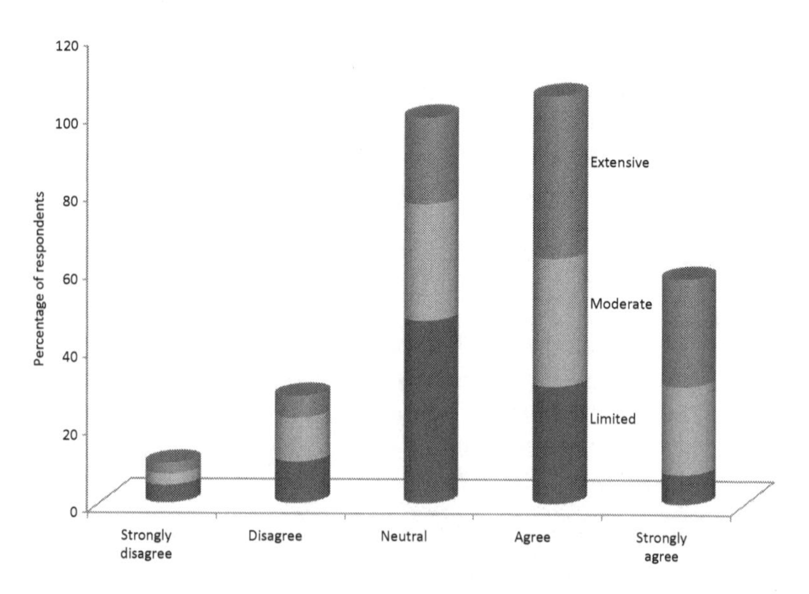

Figure 3.18 Degree of NET used and its impact-3.

Figure 3.18 shows that the pattern of opinions expressed by the respondents is different than the other two aspects. For instance, less than 50 per cent (37.9) of students of limited NET use category agreed or strongly agreed that NET use provides greater control of class activities while this percentage was more than 50 per cent in the case of first two impacts. As far as the opinion of moderate and extensive users of NET is concerned, it is similar to that of the previous two aspects. Since the pattern of opinions in different categories of NET use is dissimilar, it may be inferred that opinion is dependent on the intensity of NET use. This is captured by Chi-sq test that shows that Chi-sq statistics is significant at 10 per cent level.

The next question was whether use of digital technologies contributes to improvement in learning. The effect of learning aspects was measured on a 4-point scale, i.e. 1 'Do not use', 2 'Negative effect', 3 'No effect', 4 'Learning improved'. Although many aspects of learning were considered, the bivariate analysis focuses on the three most important aspects, namely: Use of NET helps in online sharing material among students; helps in online readings; helps in submitting assignments online. The analysis of the first aspect of learning is presented in Figure 3.19.

It can be seen from Figure 3.19 that almost two-thirds of respondents opined that use of digital technologies improves learning. Going by the various categories of NET use it is found that 65.1 per cent of limited

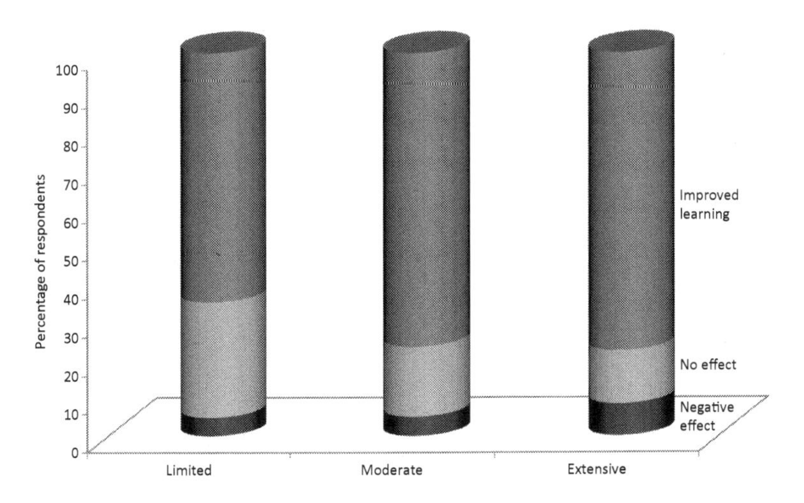

Figure 3.19 Degree of NET used and improvement in learning and class management-1.

NET users and 76.7 and 77.8 per cent of moderate and extensive users respectively of new technologies are of the view that NET use helps in online sharing of material among students. On average, 20 per cent felt that it has no effect on the learning process. The figure also shows that the opinion of respondents is similar in all categories of NET users. This is substantiated by the Chi-sq test. The insignificance of test statistics is a case in point.

The second most important learning factor emerged in the univariate analysis is NET use helps in online reading. The analysis of this aspect is presented in Figure 3.20.

Figure 3.20 shows that the pattern of responses related to this aspect is similar to that of the first. It can be seen from the figure that 86.1 per cent of extensive NET users opined that it contributes to improvement in learning. Since the distribution of opinions across various degrees of NET use is similar, the association between degree of NET use and opinion on improvement in learning is likely to be insignificant. This is captured by a Chi-squared test that shows that the test statistics are insignificant.

The third aspect of improvement in learning is the submission of assignments online. The analysis of this aspect is presented in Figure 3.21.

It can be seen from Figure 3.21 that the opinion on the third aspect is similar to other two aspects. Like in other cases, the association is insignificant. It may be inferred that students, irrespective of the degree of

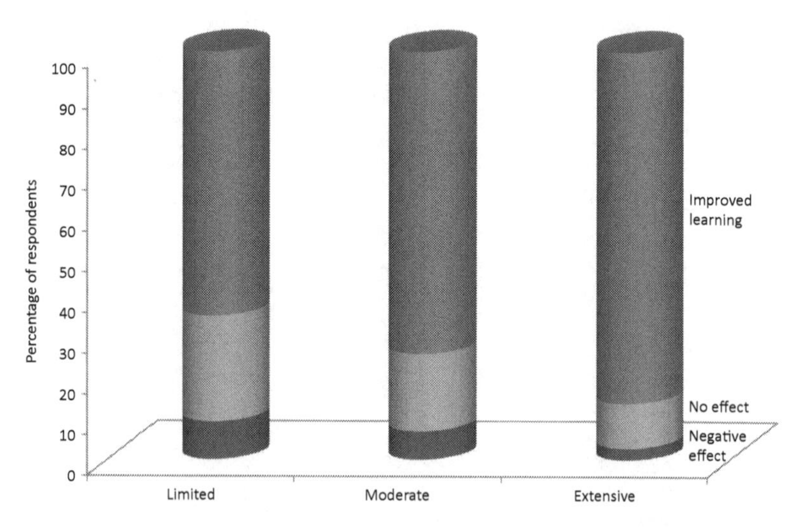

Figure 3.20 Degree of NET used and improvement in learning and class management-2.

NET use, feel that use of digital technologies improved online submission of assignments.

It was expected that job preference of students might be a factor towards influencing the NET use. To investigate this phenomenon, the preference of students on various kinds of jobs was collected. The analysis is presented in Figure 3.22.

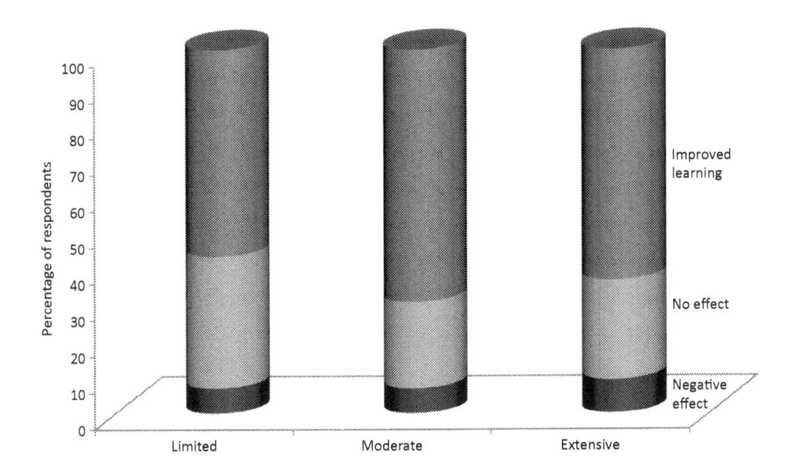

Figure 3.21 Degree of NET used and improvement in learning and class management-3.

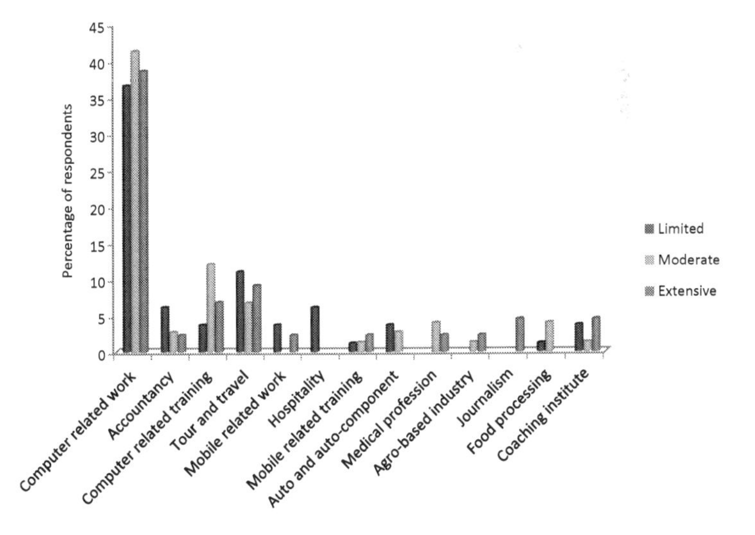

Figure 3.22 First preference of job and NET use.

It can be seen from the figure that there is no statistically significant association between job preference, and the use of digital technologies. Although a substantially high percentage of students prefer computer-related jobs, the variability within various types of NET users is very limited.

It can also be seen from Figure 3.22 that the preference of 'tour and travel' services is inversely associated with intensity of NET use, suggesting that the percentage of limited users (11.0) is higher than that of extensive users (9.1 per cent). The figure also shows that the first preference of merely five students is hospitality and they are all limited users of NET. The significant association between hospitality job and intensity of NET use suggests that students who prefer the hospitality sector do not need too many digital technologies. Hence they fall into the limited user category. The findings are on expected lines.

Multivariate analysis

Two statistical tools, namely cluster analysis and discriminant analysis, were used to analyse the degree of NET use by students.

Cluster analysis

Cluster analysis was used to group the students with similar opinions. The cluster analysis forms the clusters of observations in such a way that distance of observation is minimal within a group while it is maximal between the groups. The entire population (all the students) was grouped into three clusters.

The opinion of students on the purpose of NET use was sought on a binary scale (Yes or No). The purposes considered in the study are: Preparation of assignment, Access to library resources, Download reading material, Download class notes, Communication with teachers, Communication with other students/friends, Communication with your college/university, and to see results online. The analysis results are presented in Figure 3.23.

It can be seen from Figure 3.23 that 96 (47.7 per cent) of students have been grouped in cluster 1. The main purposes cited by the students of cluster 1 are 'Preparation of assignments' and 'Communication with teachers and university'. For the second cluster of 21 students (10.5 per cent), the main purposes are 'Access to library resources' and 'Checking of results online'. The third cluster of students are those use NET for 'Downloading reading material and class notes' and 'Communication with students'.

In the next part of the analysis, students are grouped based on the relevance of NET use. The opinions on various benefits were sought on a

4-point scale, i.e. 1 'Not useful', 2 'Neutral', 3 'Useful', 4 'Very useful'. The benefits included in the analysis are: Help in understanding concepts more clearly, Better illustration of ideas, Increased creativity, Better job prospects, Make more confident, Help in personality development, Improved learning abilities, Provides opportunity to interact with students of other institutions effectively, Equated with international teaching methodologies, Convenience, Help in managing class activities (e.g. planning, apportioning time etc.). In the same way as purposes of NET, the students are grouped into three clusters using cluster analysis. The results are presented in Figure 3.24.

Figure 3.24 shows that almost one-third of students (36.8 per cent) were classified in cluster 1. They considered NET use is either useful or very

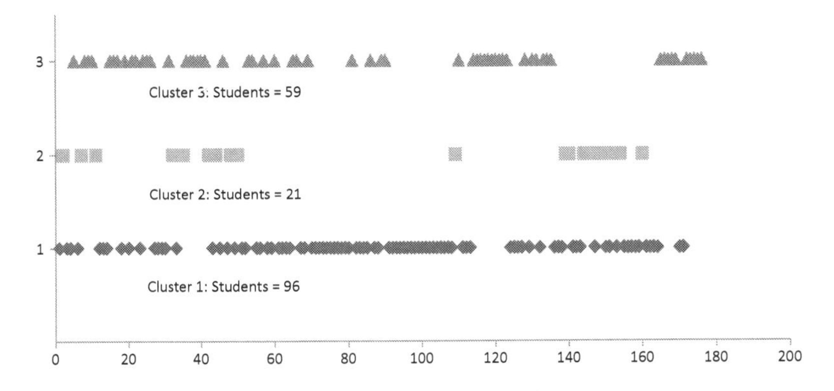

Figure 3.23 Purpose of NET use.

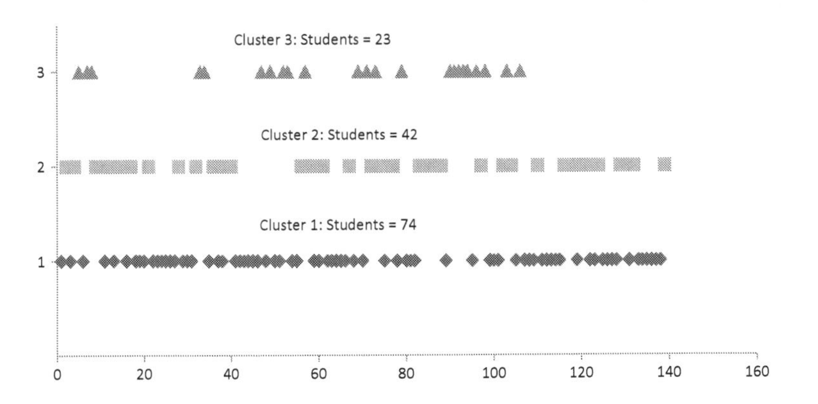

Figure 3.24 Relevance of NET use.

useful in 'Understanding concepts more clearly', 'Provides opportunity to interact with other students' and 'Helps in managing class activities more efficiently'. On the other hand, the second cluster of students (20.9 per cent) expressed the same opinion of 'Better illustration of ideas', 'Increased creativity', 'Improved learning abilities', and 'Convenience', while 11.4 per cent of students are classified in cluster 3. They considered NET use is useful or very useful with respect to 'Better job prospects', 'Made more confident', and 'Helps in personality development'.

The data were subjected to cluster analysis with respect to impact of NET use. The various impacts included 'Helps to better communicate with faculty', 'Helps to better communicate and collaborate with class mates', 'Helps in skill development', 'Results in prompt feedback from the faculty', 'Provides more opportunities for practice and reinforcement', 'More likely to focus on real-world tasks and examples', 'Allows greater control of class activities' (e.g. planning, apportioning time). The opinions were sought on a 5-point scale i.e. 1 'Strongly disagree', 2 'Disagree', 3 'Neutral', 4 'Agree', 5 'Strongly agree'. The analysis is presented in Figure 3.25.

It can be seen from Figure 3.25 that cluster 1 consists of 46.3 per cent of students who either agreed or strongly agreed with 'Helps in skill development', 'Provides more opportunities for practice and reinforcement' and 'Allows greater control of class activities'. Roughly 13 (12.9) per cent are grouped in the second cluster. These students expressed the same opinion related to two aspects, namely: use of NET 'Results in prompt feedback from the faculty' and makes the user 'More likely to focus on real-world tasks and examples'. The third cluster consists of 23.9 per cent of students who agreed or strongly agreed that use of NET 'Helps to better communicate with faculty' and 'Helps to better communicate and collaborate

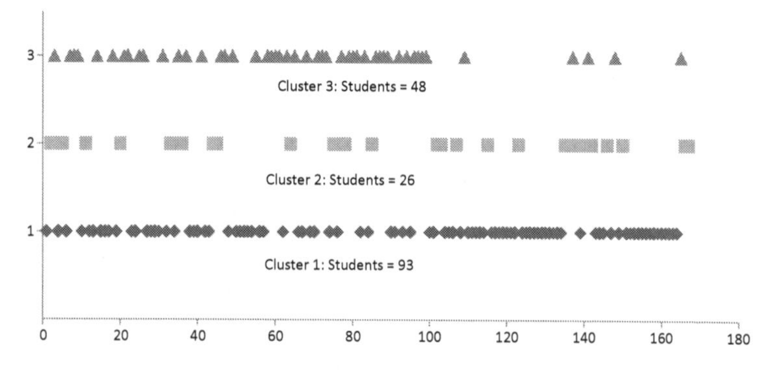

Figure 3.25 Impact.

with classmates'. It may be inferred from the analysis that a fairly large number of students viewed skill development and greater control of class activities as the major impacts.

The learning aspect of education is considered very important. Therefore, it was deemed necessary to seek the opinion of students whether the use of digital technologies contributes to improving the learning process. In this context, various aspects of learning were considered. These are: Online syllabus, Online readings, Online discussion board, Online access to sample exams, Submitting assignments online, Getting online assignments back from faculty with comments and Online sharing material among students. The opinions on these aspects were collected on 4-point scale i.e. 1 'Did not use', 2 'Negative effect', 3 'No effect' and 4 'Improved learning'. The students were grouped into three categories using cluster analysis. The results are presented in Figure 3.26.

It can be seen from Figure 3.26 that 49.3 per cent of students are grouped in first cluster. This group of students opined that improvement in learning was achieved through the availability of 'Online syllabus', 'Online access to sample exams' and 'Online sharing material among students'. The second cluster of students (23.9 per cent) think that activities such as 'Online readings' and 'Online discussion board' contributed to improvement in learning while 9.95 per cent of students (third cluster) think that 'Submitting assignments online' and 'Getting online assignments back from faculty with comments' improved their learning process. The findings presented in Figure 3.26 suggest that online activities are considered to contribute to the learning process.

The following subsection identifies the discriminating characteristics of students that led to varying degree of NET use.

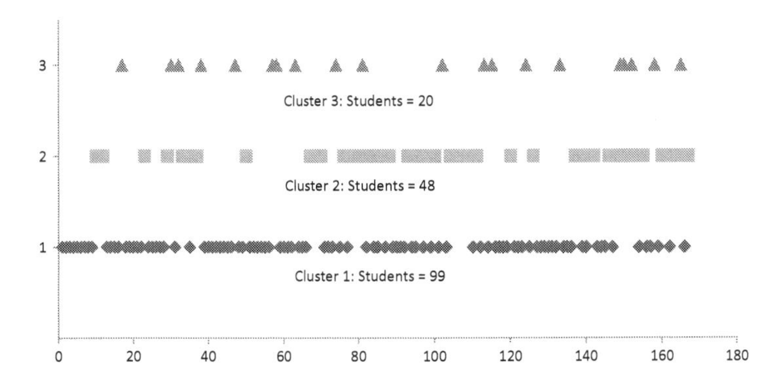

Figure 3.26 Learning.

Discriminant analysis

Subsequently the data are subjected to a multivariate test called discriminant analysis to identify factors that discriminated students on the basis of degree of NET use. Various models of the analysis were tried and tested but only the best-fit model of discriminant analysis is presented in Table 3.1.

The results show that all the variables except skill development (impact-2) and online access to syllabus (improve-1) emerged significant in discriminating the three groups of students. It can be seen from Table 3.1 that age has significantly discriminated students of three groups. The level of significance is at 1 per cent. It seems that the senior students who are pursuing research (MPhil or PhD) use NET extensively compared to others who are pursuing undergraduate or postgraduate courses. The results are not surprising as the use of NET extensively is imperative for senior students. They have to not only use NET for accessing the latest research papers but also to access databases that are necessary for their research work. The senior students need to interact more frequently with their supervisors and other researchers working on similar topics. Hence senior students might be using NET more extensively than others. The findings substantiate the first hypothesis of the study.

The table also indicates that all three factors of relevance, namely 'Better illustration of ideas', 'Better job prospects' and 'Convenience' have emerged significant in discriminating students among the three groups. The levels of significance are 5, 10 and 1 per cent respectively. This could be because the students of engineering courses in particular use the latest software that helps in expressing their ideas in a better and convenient way. The results also show that the students who are well conversant in state-of-the-art application software packages might find it easier to get ICT-related jobs. The students who are inclined towards technology oriented jobs would try to learn and use digital technologies as much as possible so that they can use the knowledge that they acquired during studies in searching for jobs. The finding is very much according to our expectation and thus the hypothesis 2, i.e. positive association between job prospects and degree of NET use, holds true.

The findings of the study suggests that the two impacts, i.e. 'Better communication and collaboration with classmates' and 'Allows greater control of class activities', emerged significant in discriminating the three groups of students. Their level of significance is 1 per cent. The emergence of these factors is according to our expectation since the use of NET enables students to integrate not only with other students but also with society in general. It enables them to share a lot of commonality and consequently provides better control in academics and other activities. On the other hand,

Table 3.1 Discriminant analysis

Variables	*Average ranking by NET user group*			*Wilk's Lambda*	F-*Stat.*	*Level of Sig.*	*Description of variables*
	I	II	III				
Rel-1	2.87	3.16	3.28	0.956	3.34	0.038	Better illustration of ideas
Rel-2	2.60	2.86	3.09	0.960	3.06	0.050	Better job prospects
Rel-3	2.75	3.19	3.41	0.922	6.16	0.003	Convenience
Impact-1	3.50	3.42	3.94	0.944	4.34	0.015	Better communication and collaboration with classmates
Impact-2	3.48	3.65	3.69	0.992	0.59	0.551	Skill development
Impact-3	3.30	3.70	3.88	0.949	3.94	0.021	Allows greater control of class activities
Age	1.57	2.00	2.19	0.883	9.63	0.000	Age of student
Financial status	1.63	1.51	1.38	0.961	2.94	0.056	Financial nature of institution
Course	3.87	4.42	5.03	0.939	4.74	0.010	Courses offered in universities
Improve-1	3.17	3.33	3.25	0.996	0.32	0.724	Online access to syllabus
Improve-2	2.55	3.13	2.91	0.955	3.42	0.035	Online access to discussion board
Improve-3	2.70	3.33	3.00	0.948	4.01	0.020	Online access to sample papers

those who use NET to a limited extent feel isolated from these students resulting in being less confident. The discriminatory nature of the second impact is also according to our expectation and very obvious. The students who use new technologies, such as e-mail with drop box facility and access resources through file transfer protocol, can communicate with other students and teachers more effectively. The NET provides them opportunity to interact through the anywhere, anyone and anytime mode. Hence the hypothesis 3 that the use of NET has noticeable impact on students holds true.

The financial status of institutions plays a significant role in discriminating the three groups of NET users. The level of significance is at 5 per cent. This could be due to the reason that researchers (MPhil and PhD) prefer public-funded institutions as the kind of digital resources required by them may not be available in privately funded universities. Since research scholars are fewer in number in any self-financed university, it may not be viable for them to acquire such technologies. Therefore research scholars prefer government institutions and use NET extensively. Although the financial nature of institutions plays a discriminatory role in NET use, the finding is not according to our expectation.

The findings about improvement in learning (Table 3.1) show that two activities, namely 'Online access to discussion board' and 'Online access to sample papers', have significantly discriminated the three groups of NET users. The level of significance is 5 per cent. However, 'Online access to syllabuses' has not emerged as significant. This could be due to the fact that all the students, irrespective of NET use, assigned high rank to this factor.

Based on the discriminant function used in the analysis, the students are regrouped according to predicted membership. The results are presented in Table 3.2.

It can be seen from the classification table that 66.7 per cent of limited users of NET have been correctly classified. The percentages of such students in moderate or extensive users of NET are 54.4 and 59.4 per cent

Table 3.2 Classification results

Original group membership	*Predicted group membership*			
	Limited	*Moderate*	*Extensive*	*Total*
Limited	40 (66.7)	14	6	60
Moderate	14	31 (54.4)	12	57
Extensive	7	6	19 (59.4)	32

Notes

Classification power of the function: 60.4 per cent.

Figures in parenthesis are correctly classified respondents.

respectively. The overall classification power of the discriminant function is 60.4 per cent, which is more than 50 per cent and considered as being within the permissible limit.

Appendix 3.1: student data analysis

Table 3.A1 Accessibility of NET

Type of technology	*Personal (%)*	*Institutional (%)*
Standalone desktop	1.0	1.0
Desktop with internet	24.9	76.6
Standalone laptop	3.5	0.5
Laptop with internet	65.2	19.9
Tablet/iPad	10.4	2.5
E-reader	8.0	10.0

Table 3.A2 Accessibility of network technologies

Type of technology	*Yes (%)*	*No (%)*
Intranet	148 (84.1)	28 (15.9)
Wi-Fi	168 (86.6)	26 (13.4)
Cloud computing	40 (19.9)	84 (41.8)

Note
Figures in parentheses are percentage of total respondents.

Table 3.A3 Relevance of digital technologies in various activities

Activities	*Score*				*Average score*
	1	*2*	*3*	*4*	
Helped in understanding concepts more clearly	4.5	10.4	40.3	32.8	3.15
Better illustration of ideas	3.5	17.9	34.3	32.3	3.08
Increased creativity	4.0	22.4	33.3	26.4	2.95
Better job prospects	6.5	24.4	24.9	26.4	2.87
Made more confident	9.0	25.4	26.9	22.4	2.75
Helped in personality development	10.4	23.4	32.3	19.9	2.72
Improved learning abilities	6.5	14.4	36.3	28.9	3.02
Provides opportunity to interact with students of other institutions effectively	10.9	22.9	26.4	21.9	2.72
Equated with international teaching methodologies	10.4	20.9	27.4	24.4	2.79
Convenience	5.0	18.9	25.9	34.8	3.07
Helped in managing class activities	6.5	17.9	31.8	21.9	2.89

Note
Figures are percentage respondents.

Table 3.A4 Impact of new technology use

Aspects	*Score*					*Average score*
	1	*2*	*3*	*4*	*5*	
Better communication with faculty	1.5	8.5	32.3	35.8	10.4	3.51
Better communication and collaboration with classmates	3.0	7.0	30.3	35.3	14.9	3.58
Skill development	2.0	9.5	31.3	35.8	12.4	3.52
Helped in prompt feedback from the faculty	4.5	11.9	33.3	27.9	8.5	3.28
Provided more opportunities for practice and reinforcement	4.5	7.5	32.8	30.8	11.9	3.44
More likely to focus on real-world tasks	3.0	11.4	24.9	33.3	12.9	3.49
Allows greater control of class activities	3.0	8.5	29.9	28.9	15.4	3.53

Note
Figures are percentage respondents.

Table 3.A5 NET use and improvement in learning and managing classes

Activities	*Score*				*Average score*
	1	*2*	*3*	*4*	
Online syllabus	15.4	5.0	17.4	48.8	3.15
Online readings	14.9	5.0	14.4	54.2	3.22
Online discussion board	22.9	7.0	21.9	35.3	2.80
Online access to sample exams	19.9	6.0	15.4	45.3	2.99
Submitting assignments online	13.9	5.5	21.9	47.3	3.16
Getting online assignments back from faculty with comments	20.9	6.0	22.4	38.3	2.89
Online sharing material among students	8.5	4.5	17.4	57.2	3.41

Note
Figures are percentage respondents.

Table 3.A6 Barriers for using e-class

Aspects	*Average score*	*Ranking*
Not very relevant	2.06	6
Do not have necessary skills	2.14	5
Do not have technical support needed	2.33	2
E-class infra is insufficient	2.51	1
E-classes are not very effective	2.20	4
Technology is not very reliable	2.32	3

Table 3.A7 Degree of NET used and course of study

Study course	*Extent of NET use*					
	Limited		*Moderate*		*Extensive*	
	No	*Col. %*	*No*	*Col. %*	*No*	*Col. %*
Traditional arts and commerce	4	4.9	6	8.0	1	2.3
Traditional science courses	24	29.3	7	9.3	2	4.5
Professional courses	–	–	–	–	2	4.5
Engineering courses	14	17.1	28	37.3	14	31.8
Management courses	34	41.5	10	13.3	7	15.9
Law	–	–	1	1.3	–	–
Research (PhD and innovation)	6	7.3	23	30.7	18	40.9
Total	82	100.0	75	100.0	44	100.0

Note
Chi-square: 61.712, Level of Sig.: 0.000.

Table 3.A8 Degree of NET used and age of students

Degree of NET used	*Age*						*Total*	
	18–20		*21–23*		*24+*			
	No	*Row %*	*No*	*Row %*	*No*	*Row %*	*No*	*Col. %*
Limited	46	56.1	30	36.6	6	7.3	82	40.8
Moderate	19	25.3	35	46.7	21	28.0	75	37.3
Extensive	10	22.7	13	29.5	21	47.7	44	21.9
Total	75	37.3	78	38.8	48	23.9	201	100.0

Note
Chi-square: 35.850, Sig.: 0.000.

Table 3.A9 Degree of NET used and financial status of the institution

Degree of NET used	*Financial status*				*Total*	
	Public funded		*Self-financed*			
	No	*Row %*	*No*	*Row %*	*No*	*Col. %*
Limited	26	31.7	56	68.3	82	40.8
Moderate	39	52.0	36	48.0	75	37.3
Extensive	28	63.6	16	36.4	44	21.9
Total	93	46.3	108	53.7	201	100.0

Note
Chi-square: 13.323, Sig.: 0.001.

Table 3.A10 Degree of NET used and its relevance-1

Degree of NET used	*Use of NET helped in understanding concepts more clearly*								*No response*	
	Not useful		*Neutral*		*Useful*		*Very useful*			
	No	*Row %*	*No*	*Row %*	*No*	*Row %*	*No*	*Row %*	*No*	*Row %*
Limited	4	4.9	14	17.1	28	34.1	22	26.8	14	17.1
Moderate	3	4.0	3	4.0	37	49.3	26	34.7	6	8.0
Extensive	2	4.5	4	9.1	16	36.4	18	40.9	4	9.1
Total	9	4.5	21	10.4	81	40.3	66	32.8	24	11.9

Note
Chi-square: 13.968, Sig.: 0.083.

Table 3.A11 Degree of NET used and its relevance-2

Degree of NET used	*Use of NET helped in better illustration of ideas*								*No response*	
	Not useful		*Neutral*		*Useful*		*Very useful*			
	No	*Row %*	*No*	*Row %*	*No*	*Row %*	*No*	*Row %*	*No*	*Row %*
Limited	4	4.9	20	24.4	17	32.9	18	22.0	13	15.9
Moderate	3	4.0	10	13.3	29	38.7	27	36.0	6	8.0
Extensive			6	13.6	13	29.5	20	45.5	5	11.4
Total	7	3.5	36	17.9	69	34.3	65	32.3	24	11.9

Note
Chi-square: 13.475, Sig.: 0.097.

Table 3.A12 Degree of NET used and its relevance-3

Degree of NET used	*Use of NET helped in convenience*								*No response*	
	Not useful		*Neutral*		*Useful*		*Very useful*			
	No	*Row %*	*No*	*Row %*	*No*	*Row %*	*No*	*Row %*	*No*	*Row %*
Limited	5	7.4	20	29.4	26	38.2	17	25.0	14	17.1
Moderate	5	7.7	11	16.9	17	26.2	32	49.2	10	13.3
Extensive	–	–	7	18.9	9	24.3	21	56.8	7	15.9
Total	10	5.8	38	22.2	52	30.4	70	40.9	31	15.4

Note
Chi-square: 16.724, Sig.: 0.033.

Table 3.A13 Degree of NET used and its impact-1

Degree of NET used	*Use of NET Provides opportunities to better communicate and collaborate with classmates*										*Total*	
	Strongly disagree		*Disagree*		*Neutral*		*Agree*		*Strongly agree*			
	No	*Row %*	*No*	*Row %*	*No*	*Row %*	*No*	*Row %*	*No*	*Row %*	*No*	*Row %*
Limited	2	2.8	8	11.1	24	33.3	33	45.8	5	6.9	10	12.2
Moderate	2	2.8	4	5.6	25	35.2	22	31.0	18	25.4	4	5.3
Extensive	2	5.1	2	5.1	12	30.8	16	41.0	7	17.9	5	11.4
Total	6	3.3	14	7.7	61	33.5	71	39.0	30	16.5	19	9.5

Note
Chi-square: 11.958, Sig.: 0.153.

Table 3.A14 Degree of NET used and its impact-2

Degree of NET used	*Use of NET helped me in skill development*										*Total*	
	Strongly disagree		*Disagree*		*Neutral*		*Agree*		*Strongly agree*			
	No	*Row %*	*No*	*Row %*	*No*	*Row %*	*No*	*Row %*	*No*	*Row %*	*No*	*Row %*
Limited	2	2.7	9	12.2	28	37.8	28	37.8	7	9.5	8	9.8
Moderate	1	1.4	7	9.9	25	35.2	29	40.8	9	12.7	4	5.3
Extensive	1	2.6	3	7.9	10	26.3	15	39.5	9	23.7	6	13.6
Total	4	2.2	19	10.4	63	34.4	72	39.3	25	13.7	18	8.9

Note
Chi-square: 5.666, Sig.: 0.685.

Table 3.A15 Degree of NET used and its impact-3

Degree of NET used	*Use of NET allows greater control of class activities*										*Total*	
	Strongly disagree		*Disagree*		*Neutral*		*Agree*		*Strongly agree*			
	No	*Row %*	*No*	*Row %*	*No*	*Row %*	*No*	*Row %*	*No*	*Row %*	*No*	*Row %*
Limited	3	4.5	7	10.6	31	47.0	20	30.3	5	7.6	16	19.5
Moderate	2	2.9	8	11.4	21	30.0	23	32.9	16	22.9	5	6.7
Extensive	1	2.8	2	5.6	8	22.2	15	41.7	10	27.8	8	18.2
Total	6	3.5	17	9.9	60	34.9	58	33.7	31	18.0	29	14.4

Note
Chi-square: 13.850, Sig.: 0.086.

Table 3.A16 Degree of NET used and improvement in learning and class management-1

Degree of NET used	*Use of NET helped in online sharing material among students*						*No response*	
	Negative effect		*No effect*		*Improved learning*			
	No	*Row %*	*No*	*Row %*	*No*	*Row %*	*No*	*Row %*
Limited	3	4.8	19	30.2	41	65.1	19	23.2
Moderate	3	5.0	11	18.3	46	76.7	15	20.0
Extensive	3	8.3	5	13.9	28	77.8	8	18.2
Total	9	5.7	35	22.0	115	72.3	42	20.9

Note
Chi-square: 5.166, Sig.: 0.523.

Table 3.A17 Degree of NET used and improvement in learning and class management-2

Degree of NET used	*Use of NET helped in online readings*						*No response*	
	Negative effect		*No effect*		*Improved learning*			
	No	*Row %*	*No*	*Row %*	*No*	*Row %*	*No*	*Row %*
Limited	5	9.3	14	25.9	35	64.8	28	34.1
Moderate	4	6.9	11	19.0	43	74.1	17	22.7
Extensive	1	2.8	4	11.1	31	86.1	8	18.2
Total	10	6.8	29	19.6	109	73.6	53	26.4

Note
Chi-square: 9.333, Sig.: 0.156.

Table 3.A18 Degree of NET used and improvement in learning and class management-3

Degree of NET used	*Use of NET helped in submitting assignments online*						*No response*	
	Negative effect		*No effect*		*Improved learning*			
	No	*Row %*	*No*	*Row %*	*No*	*Row %*	*No*	*Row %*
Limited	4	6.9	21	36.2	33	56.9	24	29.3
Moderate	4	6.8	14	23.7	41	69.5	16	21.3
Extensive	3	9.1	9	27.3	21	63.6	11	25.0
Total	11	7.3	44	29.3	95	63.3	51	25.4

Note
Chi-square: 6.142, Sig.: 0.631.

Table 3.A19 First preference of job and NET use

First preference of job	*Extent of NET use*			*Chi-square [Sig.]*	*Total respondents*
	Limited	*Moderate*	*Extensive*		
Computer-related work	36.6	41.3	38.6	0.944	78
Accountancy	6.1	2.7	2.3	4.788	8
Computer-related training	3.7	12.0	6.8	4.876	15
Tour and travel	11.0	6.7	9.1	2.535	18
Mobile-related work	3.7	–	2.3	5.131	4
Hospitality	6.1	–	–	8.029*	5
Mobile-related training	1.2	1.3	2.3	1.086	3
Auto and auto-component	3.7	2.7	–	4.173	5
Medical profession	–	4.0	2.3	5.019	4
Agro-based industry	–	1.3	2.3	5.171	2
Journalism	–	–	4.5	9.357*	2
Food processing	1.2	4.0	–	3.585	4
Coaching institute	3.7	1.3	4.5	3.028	6

Note

Figures are percentage to total respondents; *→ Significant at 10% level.

4 Adoption of digital technologies in tertiary education[1]

Introduction

Education is not only an instrument for enhancing efficiency but is also an effective tool for upgrading the overall intellectual capability of individuals. Education improves functional and investigative ability thereby opening up opportunities for individuals to achieve greater access to labour markets and livelihoods since a better-educated labour force is essential to meet the labour supply requirements for faster growth. Skills and knowledge are the engines of economic growth and social development of any country. Countries that have higher and better levels of knowledge and skills respond more effectively and promptly to the challenges and opportunities of globalization.

The higher education outcome is reflected in the transformation of individuals in their knowledge, characteristics and behaviour. Universities across the globe have realized that their long-term survival depends on how good their services are and that quality of education sets one university apart from the rest (Aly & Akpovi, 2001; Tsinidou et al. 2010; Goel, 2015). The paradigm shift from industrial society to information society had already become a reality. It is indeed high time to think about integrating digital technologies in all facets of education. The integration of digital technologies in higher education will prompt several broader innovations. Technology-based teaching and learning strategies may open possibilities for designing new curricula and new methods of assessment to meet our educational objectives (Jattan & Chaudhary, 2015).

The digital technologies in higher education are ubiquitous. They can be applied in managerial functions in academic institutions or for knowledge acquisition and dissemination among the students. The technologies when applied to the teaching process can significantly change the traditional education. Some examples of these information technologies in education include computer technologies used to generate course materials such as word processing, presentation programs, database programs, electronic mails, websites, blogs, social networking sites etc. Information systems used to manage various courses such as course management systems or LMS are other examples of tertiary-level educational technology (Roblyer, 2006; Mangin, 2011; John 2015). There has been rapid adoption of these technologies in Indian HEIs. However, it is less known for what purpose these new technologies are being used by these institutions. Irrespective of the purpose of the use of digital technologies, a strong and reliable physical and technological infrastructure is essential for successful use of new technologies. The earlier research has taken place on the impact of ICT use in higher education. Earlier researchers have attempted to explore only limited aspects of use of digital technology in tertiary education. This study, on the other hand, focuses on different aspects such as its purpose, impact, relevance and improvement in learning by the use of digital technologies.

Review of literature

This section includes some relevant studies undertaken in the use of network technologies. Some studies carried out on various aspects of new technologies are presented in separate sub-sections.

Purpose and impact of digital technologies

Mashhadia and Kargozari (2011) found that digital classrooms are considered as the vital element in promoting and improving the traditional methods of teaching and learning. Digital classes transform the education process and cause universal interactivity between students and their faculty all around the world. This global interactivity causes mutual understanding among students and faculty. Kirschner and Woperies (2003) concludes that ICT can make the higher education institutions more efficient and productive by organizing a variety of tools to enhance and facilitate users' professional activities. Another study by Soloway and Pryor (1996) concludes that the pervasive influence of ICT has brought about a rapid technological, social, political and economic transformation, which has paved the way to a network society, organized around ICT in the field of higher education. Adeoye et al. (2013) in their study on six tertiary educational institutions in South West Nigeria found that use of ICT in these institutions is necessary in order to create opportunities for the institutions to communicate with one another through e-mail, mailing lists and chat rooms, and provides easier access to more extensive and current information.

Jattan and Chaudhary (2015) in their study on 250 students from various state universities of Haryana, India found that the students were very enthusiastic towards the use of ICT in their curricula and were oriented towards developing skills to learn various computer programs and the majority of students use computers and browsed information on the Internet. Barnaghi and Sheth (2014) found that there is a rapid adoption of internet-enabled devices in HEIs that facilitate web browsing and communication across borders. Yusuf and Onasany (2004) opined that ICT provides opportunities for users to communicate with one another through e-mail, mailing lists, chat rooms and other facilities. It provides quicker and easier access to more extensive and current information. ICT can also be used to perform complex tasks as it provides researchers with a steady avenue for the dissemination of research reports and findings.

Relevance and improvement in learning through digital technologies

Ibrahim (2014), in his research on HEIs in Nigeria, found that ICTs provide innumerable benefits in enriching the quality and quantity of teaching/learning processes in these institutions. A study by Mashhadia and Kargozari (2011) concludes that different educational organizations enter a competitive situation for promoting their materials and methods, and the result is the improvement of learning and educational processes. Digital classrooms also reduce the gap of qualification and knowledge of students in different geographical areas. Timesaving is one of the most important consequences of digital classrooms on education.

A study by Young (2002) found that students are appreciating the capability to undertake education anywhere and anytime through the use of educational technologies. This flexibility has heightened the availability of just-in-time learning and provided learning opportunities for many more learners who previously were constrained by other commitments. Sosin et al. (2004) constructed a database of 67 sections of introductory economics, enrolling 3986 students, taught by 30 instructors in 15 institutions in the United States of America during the spring and autumn semesters of 2002. They found significant, but low, positive impact on student performance as a result of ICT use. But they showed that ICT seems to be positively correlated to performance. Fuchs and Woesmann (2004) used international data from the Program for International Students' Assessment (PISA). They showed that the bivariate correlation between the availability of ICT and students' performance is strong and significantly positive.

Objectives and hypotheses

The digital environment helps students to share their ideas and experiences. It also aids in communication with other students and teachers. Digital technologies comprises all forms of electronically supported learning and teaching tools in tertiary education. The computer and network-enabled transfer of skills and knowledge serve as tools to improve the learning process. The integration of technology into classrooms is an approach to develop better understanding of basic concepts. The main objective of this study is to investigate the factors that influence the degree of adoption of NET. The factors can be broadly categorized into purpose of use, its relevance, impact on students, improvement in learning and job preference of students. The main research questions of the study are:

1 Is the NET use in higher education relevant for students?
2 Does digital technology have potential to help students in improving their creativity and understanding more complex concepts easily?
3 Does the use of network technologies impact students' job prospects?

Based on the literature survey and in view of the research questions of the study, the following hypotheses have been formulated:

The students use digital technologies for various reasons. The different purposes could range from downloading reading materials, accessing results to communicating with faculty and other students. An earlier study by Fuchs and Woesmann (2004) found that ICT use helps students exploit enormous possibilities for acquiring information for teaching purposes and can increase learning through communication. It helps students in enhancing learning processes by making it less dependent on differing teacher quality and by making education available at home throughout the day. Furthermore, authors argue that the use of ICT can transmit knowledge to students expeditiously. Having some knowledge of the nature of association between purpose and digital technologies, it is hypothesized that purpose may play an important role in influencing intensity of NET use.

H1: The purposes are likely to influence the degree of NET adoption

The technological advancements have transformed higher education tremendously and its importance in students' life is undisputed. A study by

Afari-Kumah and Tanye (2009) concludes that ICT provides a deeper understanding to students to what is taught. This is so because students' use of ICT would enhance their competence and confidence. However, many students still patronize traditional book materials as a source of information in universities rather than ICT that is more efficient and reliable. Wilson et al. (2014), in their study of 1500 students of University of Education, Winneba, Ghana, on the ability of digital technologies to support students' learning, find use of ICT to be a powerful tool that helps to address educational problems, support difficult learning activities and enhances thinking skills. Thus it is hypothesized that relevance of digital technologies might influence its use by students.

H2: Various components of relevance of NET use is expected to influence the degree of NET use

Due to the versatility of NET, the students' perception about its influence might give some interesting outcome as technology as a tool provides a wide array of hardware and software that extends learners' capability. In this context, Ibrahim (2014), in the study on Nigerian HEIs, highlights that ICT plays a significant role in the Nigerian education system. Its application in students' learning processes enhances the delivery and access to knowledge. It also brings about improvement in curriculum and produces rich outcomes in learning compared to educational systems without ICT. It encourages critical thinking and offers unlimited means of achieving educational goals. In view of such thoughts, it is hypothesized that

H3: The use of NET is likely to impact the students positively

NET is expected to provide opportunities for flexible learning, as courses and other related information are always available and accessible to students. This could increase opportunities for students' constructed learning and they might be encouraged to develop their problem-solving skills that might promote their creativity. A study by Lopez (2003) highlights the benefits of ICT in enhancing learning outcomes for students. The study found that ICT use offers a constructive approach to learning through the provision of interactive learning as such teaching and learning processes increase students' academic performance. Thus the fourth hypothesis is:

H4: The use of digital technologies is expected to contribute positively towards learning

The use of innovative technologies in higher education might lead to better skill of an individual. Ibrahim (2014) in his study concludes that ICT provides opportunities for students to gain valuable computer skills that are suitable in today's job market as technology can be used as a ready means of preparing students today for future workplaces. Students as future employees would be equipped with the requisite competence and knowledge to use ICT within their work, thereby increasing the preparation of students for most careers and vocations. Thus it is hypothesized that students' orientation about course option might depend upon their job preference.

H5: The students whose preference is technology oriented jobs are likely to use more advanced digital technologies

Conceptual framework

The various factors influencing the use of NET is depicted in Figure 4.1. There are different reasons for using digital technologies, such as its purpose, perceived impact, relevance, improvement in learning, etc. The various purposes of using digital technologies would be academic and non-academic in nature. The students are expected to use digital technologies depending upon their requirement. The perceived impact of using NET by the students could be enormous as it allows them to better communicate with counterparts and faculty.

The relevance of digital technologies in higher education is also expected to influence the intensity of NET use. The relevance of digital technologies have taken pivotal role in its diffusion due to development of function-specific tools. Another aspect, i.e. improvement in learning, is also associated with intensity of NET use because the students using online technologies provide opportunities for collaborative and cooperative learning. The job preference is also expected to influence the intensity of NET use positively as the students whose preference is technology oriented jobs might be interested in learning digital technologies during their course of study. The study uses the analytical framework as depicted in Figure 4.1.

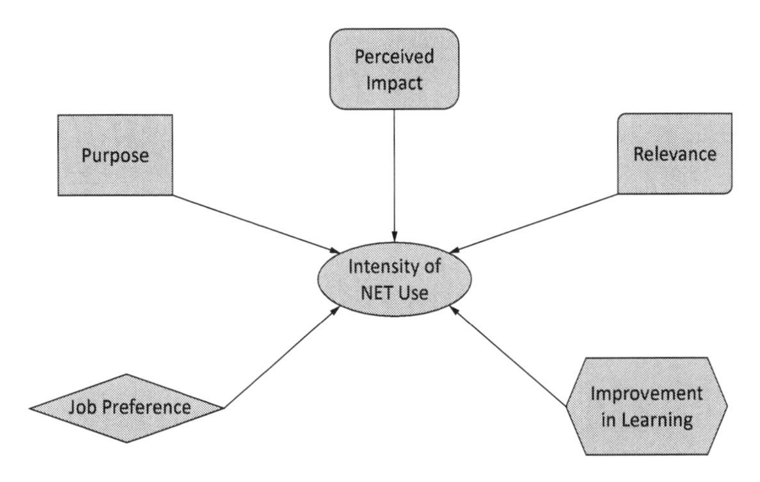

Figure 4.1 Analytical framework.

Methodology

Different analytical techniques such as univariate, bivariate and multivariate have been applied. The financial constraints did not permit having a bigger sample. Robustness of the findings may be established by future research with a substantially larger sample size.

The students have been categorized based on the extent of NET used. They are grouped as limited, moderate and extensive NET users. The students who use NET for e-mails and Internet are considered as limited users. The moderate users are those students who use digital technologies for the above reasons in addition to online activities. On the other hand, extensive users are categorized as those who use NET for the above two reasons in addition to most class activities online. The different factors that are expected to influence the degree of NET adoption are: purpose of use, relevance, its impact, improvement in learning and job preference.

The digital technologies are used for various purposes by the students. Their opinions were sought on a binary scale (Yes '1' and No '2'). Among the sample institutions, four are owned by the government (University of Delhi, Jawaharlal Nehru University, Jamia Millia Islamia, and Gautam Buddha University) and three are self-financed (Northap, Ansal and Symbiosis International University). The course of study including their codes are: Traditional Arts and Commerce '1', Traditional Science '2', Professional courses like media '3', Engineering '4', Management '5', Law '6' and Research scholars '7'. Some specific purposes of NET use included in the study are: for preparation of assignment, accessing library resources, downloading reading material, downloading class notes, communicating with teachers, communicating with other students and friends, communicating with college/university and to see results.

The importance of digital technologies for the students is innumerable. The utility of NET for the students are studied through 11 relevant factors, namely: helps in understanding concepts more clearly, contributes in better illustration of ideas, increases creativity, helps in better job prospects, makes the student more confident, helps in personality development, improves learning abilities, provides opportunity to interact with students of other institutions effectively, equates with international teaching methodologies, convenience in use and helps in managing class activities. The responses for all 11 factors of relevance of digital technologies are collected on 4-point scale, i.e. 1 'not useful', 2 'neutral', 3 'useful' and 4 'very useful'.

The next dimension of the study is the perceived impact of use of NET. The opinion of students were sought on a 5-point scale, namely: 1 'strongly disagree', 2 'disagree', 3 'neutral', 4 'agree', 5 'strongly agree'. The seven different aspects included in the study are: helping in better communication with faculty, helping in better communication and collaboration with classmates, skill development, helping in prompt feedback from the faculty, providing more opportunities for practice and reinforcement, helping to focus on real-world tasks and allowing greater control of class activities. The next factor is contributions of NET use in improving learning and managing class activities. Some of the activities used to study this aspect are: access to online syllabus, readings, discussion board, and sample exams, submitting assignments online, getting back online assignments from faculty with comments and online sharing of material among students. The opinion of students on this aspect was sought on a 4-point scale, i.e. 1 'not useful', 2 'neutral', 3 'useful' and 4 'very useful'. The next dimension expected to influence the use of NET is the job preference of students. The students were asked to rank their job preferences among the following choices, namely, computer-related work, accountancy, computer-related training, tour and travel, mobile-related work, hospitality, mobile-related training, auto and auto-component, medical profession, agro-based industry, journalism, food processing and coaching institute job.

Statistical analyses

The data collected from seven HEIs in NCR have been analysed at two levels. At the first level, the data were subjected to factor analysis. The factor analysis is also known as variable reduction technique. It is useful in two situations. First, to reconstruct the result from the original data by identifying a small number of orthogonal factors that explain most of the variance observed in much larger number of variables. And second, to screen variables for subsequent analysis, like for performing regression analysis. In this study, factor analysis has been used to generate common factors from the original variables.

At the second level, the data was subjected to Ordered Probit analysis. This statistical technique is used when a dependent variable has ordered values. The present study has the dependent variable (degree of NET use) consisting of ordered values, i.e. 1, 2 and 3. Hence Ordered Probit is preferred over other regression techniques. The original variables in the Probit model could not be used due to a multi-collinearity problem among the independent variables. This problem is taken care of by the factor analysis because factors generated using original data are orthogonal in nature.

Descriptive statistics

The distribution of students according to gender indicates 64.2 per cent are males while 35.8 per cent are females. Most of the students (38.8 per cent) are in the age group of 21–23 years. And 37.3 and 23.9 per cent belonged to the age group of 18–20 and 24+ years respectively. As far as distribution of students by their study stream is concerned, 27.9 per cent belong to engineering and 23.4 per cent are research scholars (MPhil or PhD). The students pursuing management courses represent 25.4 per cent while 16.4 and 5.5 per cent belonged to the science and arts and commerce stream respectively. Merely 1.0 and 0.5 per cent are pursuing professional courses and law respectively. The professional courses include media and nursing.

The responses for the query pertaining to the degree of NET use were collected on a 3-point scale, i.e. 1 'limited users', 2 'moderate users' and 3 'extensive users'. The results show that around 40 per cent (40.8 per cent) of respondents used NET to a limited extent while just 21.9 per cent are found to be the extensive users of the new technologies. The percentage of moderate users of NET is 37.3 per cent.

Multivariate analysis

The average of all the variables by NET use is presented in Tables 4.1 and 4.2. It can be seen from Table 4.1 that there is association between the course being pursued and the intensity of NET use. Most of the students of engineering and management courses and research scholars are extensive users of digital technologies while the majority of students pursuing art

Table 4.1 Mean values of course, financial status, purpose, relevance and degree of NET used

Variables	*Average by degree of NET used*				F-*value*	*Sig.*	*Label*
	Limited	*Moderate*	*Extensive*	*Total*			
Course	3.90	4.65	5.18	4.46	8.22	0.00	Course pursuing
FS	1.68	1.48	1.36	1.54	7.02	0.00	Financial status
Purpose of use of digital technologies							
P1	1.39	1.23	1.23	1.29	3.18	0.04	Preparation of assignment
P2	1.74	1.29	1.25	1.47	26.66	0.00	Accessing library resources
P3	1.56	1.12	1.07	1.29	33.16	0.00	Downloading reading material
P4	1.57	1.47	1.40	1.49	1.77	0.17	Downloading class notes
P5	1.57	1.60	1.20	1.50	11.00	0.00	Communicating with teachers
P6	1.74	1.35	1.20	1.48	25.84	0.00	Communicating with other students and friends
P7	1.77	1.65	1.32	1.63	14.17	0.00	Communicating with college/university
P8	1.68	1.35	1.18	1.45	20.17	0.00	To see results
Relevance of digital technologies							
R1	3.00	3.25	3.25	3.15	1.92	1.49	Helps in understanding concepts more clearly
R2	2.86	3.16	3.36	3.08	5.01	0.01	Contributes in better illustration of ideas
R3	2.78	3.01	3.16	2.95	2.63	0.07	Increases creativity
R4	2.63	2.94	3.17	2.87	4.12	0.02	Helps in better job prospects
R5	2.45	2.97	2.95	2.76	5.63	0.00	Makes the students more confident
R6	2.52	2.85	2.84	2.72	3.97	0.02	Helps in personality development
R7	2.79	3.21	3.13	3.03	5.14	0.01	Improves learning abilities
R8	2.42	2.89	2.97	2.72	5.13	0.01	Provides opportunity to interact with students of other institutions effectively
R9	2.53	2.84	3.19	2.79	5.57	0.00	Equates with international teaching methodologies
R10	2.81	3.20	3.38	3.08	5.45	0.00	Convenience in use
R11	2.64	3.04	3.26	2.92	5.33	0.00	Helps in managing class activities

and commerce courses are limited users of NET. The association between course and the extent of NET use is statistically significant at the 1 per cent level. As far as the financial status of the institution is concerned, the extensive NET users are more in public-funded than self-financed universities. The association is significant at the highest level (1 per cent).

The mean value of different purposes of NET use is presented in Table 4.1. It can be seen from the table that the average value of P1 in limited NET users' category is 1.39, which is more than the average value in the other two categories. It may be inferred that limited users have more respondents who opined that 'Preparation of assignment' is not their main purpose of NET use while it is the other way round in the other two categories of NET users. Hence it may be inferred that there is association between this purpose and intensity of NET use. Table 4.1 shows the association is statistically significant at the 5 per cent level. The similar association exists between NET use and purposes P2, P3, P5, P6, P7 and P8. Thus Hypothesis 1 i.e. *Purposes are likely to influence the degree of NET adoption* stands true.

The introduction of digital technologies in education has transformed higher education tremendously and its relevance is globally accepted. However the relevance of new technologies may not be uniform as it is influenced by the socio-economic condition of the nation. The present study seeks to investigate the relevance in Indian context. The average value of responses for all 11 factors of relevance of digital technologies is presented in Table 4.1. The result indicates that the average value of R1 in moderate and extensive category of users is more than limited users. It may be inferred that there are more students in the moderate and extensive category who assigned value 4 to this factor of relevance than the users in limited category. However the association is statistically insignificant. The table shows that in most of other factors of relevance, a higher number of students of extensive users' category assigned value 4 than in other categories of users. Hence the average value is highest in the extensive users' category. The association between various factors of relevance and the degree of NET use is statistically significant except R1.

The multivariate statistics of other indicators, i.e. perceived impact and improvement in learning is presented in Table 4.2. The table indicates that the opinion regarding I3 (skill development) is uniform across all categories of NET users. This is reflected by the almost similar average values of I3 in all groups. It may be inferred from the result that skill development has been rated very high among all the students irrespective of the intensity of NET used. The table also shows that mean values of all the factors of impact except I3 in moderate and extensive users' is higher than limited category suggesting that more extensive users of NET

Table 4.2 Mean values of impact, improvement in learning and degree of NET used

Variables	*Average by degree of NET used*				F-*value*	*Sig.*	*Label*
	Limited	*Moderate*	*Extensive*	*Total*			
Perceived impact of NET use							
I1	3.37	3.46	3.89	3.51	4.70	0.01	Better communication with faculty
I2	3.43	3.70	3.62	3.58	1.48	0.23	Better communication and collaboration with classmates
I3	3.39	3.54	3.74	3.52	1.75	0.17	Skill development
I4	3.27	3.36	3.20	3.29	0.32	0.72	Prompt feedback from the faculty
I5	3.20	3.60	3.59	3.44	3.53	0.03	Provides more opportunities for practice and reinforcement
I6	3.21	3.69	3.78	3.52	5.23	0.00	Focus on real-world tasks
I7	3.26	3.61	3.86	3.53	4.77	0.01	Allows greater control of class activities
Improvement in learning							
L1	3.11	3.34	2.95	3.16	1.50	0.23	Online syllabus
L2	2.94	3.35	3.49	3.22	3.74	0.03	Online readings
L3	2.55	3.08	2.79	2.80	3.21	0.04	Online discussion board
L4	2.70	3.37	2.90	2.99	5.41	0.01	Online sample exams
L5	3.07	3.35	3.05	3.17	1.41	0.25	Submitting assignments online
L6	2.91	2.94	2.83	2.90	0.01	0.91	Getting back online assignments from faculty with comments
L7	3.31	3.51	3.43	3.41	0.72	0.49	Online sharing of material among students

assigned value 4 to these impacts. Although the trend is similar for all the factors of impact, the association is statistically significant only in I1, I5, I6 and I7.

The use of new technologies in education is expected to contribute positively towards improvement in learning. The average value of improvement in learning is presented in Table 4.2. Three aspects of learning, namely, online readings (L2), discussion boards (L3) and sample exams (L4) have statistically significant association with the degree of NET use. The mean values for L3 and L4 are highest for moderate users and that of L2 is highest for extensive users, suggesting that the students assigned higher weightage to these aspects of learning. The mean values for the rest of the aspects of learning do not have much variation among the different groups of NET users, consequently the mean values for moderate and extensive users are almost same. Since the average value of scores is around 3, it may be inferred that most of the students are neutral with regard to improvement in learning in these aspects.

Subsequently the data were subjected to factor analysis to reduce the number of independent variables and to get rid of the multi-collinearity problem. All factors whose eigenvalue is more than 1 were retained. The analysis identified 13 such factors. Each factor represents a certain group of original variables. For instance, all the variables representing purpose of NET use are grouped into three factors. The Purpose 1 factor consist of: 'Accessing library resources', 'Downloading reading material', 'Communication with other students and friends' and 'To see results' while Purpose 2 encompasses 'Preparation of assignment', 'Communicating with teachers' and 'Communicating with college/university'. Purpose 3 consists of 'Downloading class notes'. The description of all the factors is presented in Appendix II. The score of all the factors were generated in factor analysis and are used as independent variables along with courses being pursued by the students and financial status of the institutions in regression analysis. The parameter estimates along with level of significance are presented in Table 4.3.

It can be seen from Table 4.3 that the intensity of NET use by the students is positively influenced by the course they choose. The findings are according to our expectation as the students of engineering and management courses are expected to be extensive users of digital technologies. Similarly, research scholars were also found to be extensive users of NET. The coefficient is statistically significant at the 10 per cent level.

The results show that the relevance of digital technologies significantly influences the intensity of its use. The Relevance-1 representing 'Helps in understanding concepts more clearly', 'Contributes in better illustration of ideas', 'Increases creativity', 'Helps in better job prospects', 'Improves

Table 4.3 Degree of NET use (Ordered Probit model)

Variables	*Z-statistics*	*Sig.*	*Label*
Course	1.80	0.072	Course
Financial Status	–0.96	0.335	Financial status
Factor 1	3.06	0.002	Relevance 1
Factor 2	0.99	0.321	Impact 1
Factor 3	1.77	0.077	Job 1
Factor 4	–3.16	0.002	Purpose 1
Factor 5	0.28	0.782	Learning 1
Factor 6	–0.96	0.337	Purpose 2
Factor 7	–1.75	0.081	Job 2
Factor 8	0.51	0.608	Job 3
Factor 9	–1.93	0.053	Relevance 2
Factor 10	–0.86	0.391	Job 4
Factor 11	–0.85	0.397	Learning 2
Factor 12	2.04	0.041	Relevance 3
Factor 13	–2.76	0.006	Purpose 3

Note
Dependent Variable = Degree of NET_USE.

learning abilities', 'Provides opportunity to interact with students of other institutions effectively', 'Equates with international teaching methodologies' and 'Convenience in use' positively influenced the degree of NET use at 1 per cent level of significance. Similarly Relevance-3 representing 'Helpful in managing class activities' also positively influenced the intensity of NET use with 5 per cent level of significance. This positive and significant association suggests that students think the use of latest technologies makes them more creative, improves learning abilities, etc.

This finding has been substantiated by previous studies. For instance, Mondal and Mete (2012) argued that the integration of ICTs in higher education helps in developing 'knowledge societies'. The call of the hour is the need to provide education for everyone, anywhere and anytime. Life-long learning has become the driving force to sustain in the contemporary competitive environment. Therefore to strengthen and/or advance this knowledge-driven growth, new technologies, skills and capabilities are needed. Thus the hypothesis 2 i.e. *Various components of relevance of NET use is expected to influence the degree of NET use* stands true.

Table 4.2 also shows that Relevance-2 encompassing 'Makes the students more confident' and 'Helps in personality development' significantly influenced degree of NET use with the negative sign. The negative sign suggests there is an inverse relationship between degree of NET use and opinion expressed by the users on Relevance-2. It may be inferred from the findings that moderate and extensive users do not think the NET use makes them confident nor does it contributes towards personality development. Consequently they assigned lower weight to these factors of relevance.

It was found that Factor 4 and 13, that deal with purpose of NET use by the students, negatively but significantly influences the degree of NET use. The negative sign could be due to the measurement of these variables. The value '2' is assigned for those who do not use digital technologies for these purposes while '1' is assigned for those who use. The results presented in Table 4.1 show that there are a higher number of moderate and extensive users who use digital technologies for various purposes such as 'Downloading reading material, class notes', 'Accessing library material' etc. On the other hand, the number of students who use these technologies are fewer in numbers in the limited category of users. The multivariate analysis substantiates the findings of univariate analysis. Hence Hypothesis 1 i.e. *The purposes are likely to influence the degree of NET adoption* holds true.

It can be seen from Table 4.3 that impact factor consisting of 'Better communication and collaboration with classmates', 'Skill development', 'Prompt feedback from the faculty', 'Provides more opportunities for practice and reinforcement', 'Focus on real-world tasks' and 'Allows greater control of class activities' did not emerge significant in influencing the degree of NET use. This could be due to the fact that all the students assigned high rank to these impacts irrespective of their level of NET use. This is substantiated by the average value (more than three) of the opinions presented in Table 4.2. Another study (Youssef & Dahmani, 2008) on HEIs in the European Union supports the finding. The authors highlight resource-based learning and access to real-world information through the Web, improves class activities and improved students' quality of work that has given them the confidence to perform enhanced learning tasks. The findings are according to our expectation and Hypothesis 3 i.e. *The use of NET is likely to impact the students positively* stands true.

The study includes two factors of improvement in learning. First factor (Factor 5) comprises of 'Online syllabus', 'Online readings', 'Online discussion board', 'Online sample exams', 'Submitting assignments online' and 'Getting back online assignments from faculty with comments'. The opinions expressed by the students are similar to that of impact factor, i.e. irrespective of the degree of NET use, all the students opined that NET use improves in learning. Since the opinion is independent of NET use, the first learning factor did not emerge significant in influencing NET use though the relationship is positive. On the other hand, the second factor (Factor 11) representing 'Online sharing of material among students' is negatively associated with degree of NET use. The association is insignificant. Therefore hypothesis 4 i.e. *Use of digital technologies is expected to contribute positively towards learning* does not hold true.

The study considered 14 types of jobs, namely, computer-related work, accountancy, computer-related training, tour and travel, mobile-related work, hospitality, mobile-related training, auto and auto-component, medical profession, journalism, food processing and teaching, agro-based industry and any other job. Out of the four factors retained by the factor analysis, the first factor (Factor 3), consisting of 'accountancy', 'tour and travel', 'hospitality', 'auto and auto-component' and 'agro-based industry' emerged significant in influencing the degree of NET use. Some of the above jobs require intensive use of ICTs and hence students who prefer these jobs try to learn as many computer applications as possible. Therefore the association between the job preference (Factor 3) and intensity of NET use is positively significant. It may thus be inferred that Hypothesis 5 – *Students whose preference is technology oriented jobs are likely to use more advanced digital technologies* holds true.

Summary and conclusions

This study focuses on the factors that influence the degree of adoption of NET in HEIs. The seven HEIs located in National Capital Region (NCR), India are included in the study. They are: University of Delhi, Delhi; Jawaharlal Nehru University, Delhi; Jamia Millia Islamia University, Delhi; Gautam Buddha University, Greater NOIDA; Northcap University, Gurgaon; Ansal University, Gurgaon; and Symbiosis International University, NOIDA. The survey of these universities was conducted during July 2015 to October 2016. The sample consisted of 201 students and the data were collected using a semi-structured questionnaire. Different analytical techniques have been applied to investigate the factors affecting the intensity of NET use.

Some of the factors that are taken into consideration are purpose, relevance, impact, improvement in learning and job preference of students in these universities. The extent of digital technologies used by the students is defined as the intensity of NET used. It has been measured on a 3-point scale, i.e. limited, moderate and extensive NET users. The students who use NET for e-mails, Internet and limited use for class activities are categorized as limited users. The moderate users are those students who use digital technologies for the above reasons in addition to online activities. On the other hand, extensive users are labelled as those who use NET for the above two reasons in addition to most class activities online.

The results indicate that almost all purposes of NET used by the students are statistically significant except one purpose, i.e. 'downloading class notes'. It is also found that a higher number of extensive users use digital technologies for these purposes than limited users. The Ordered Probit result indicates an inverse relationship between purpose and the different groups of NET users. The inverse relationship is due to the measurement (1 'Yes' and 2 'No') of these variables. The study finds evidence of strong and positive association between use of digital technologies with variables included in Relevance-1 and Relevance-3 factors. This positive association is because students opined that use of latest technologies makes them more creative, improves learning abilities etc.

This study finds evidence of significant impact on students due to use of digital technologies. The statistical model shows that the association between use of digital technologies and Impact-1 is positive but insignificant. The reason for insignificance is that there is no variation of opinion among different types of NET users even though all the students, irrespective of their degree of NET use, have assigned very high rank. The present study finds evidence of positive association between degree of NET use and job preference. The students whose preferences are ICT-intensive jobs are found to be extensive users of NET.

Note

1 This chapter has been published in the *Journal of Educational Technology Systems*.

References

Adeoye, Y. M., Oluwole, A. F., & Blessing, L. A. (2013). Appraising the role of information communication technology (ICT) as a change agent for higher education in Nigeria. *International Journal of Educational Administration and Policy Studies*, 5(8), 177–183.

Afari-Kumah, E., & Tanye, H. A. (2009). Tertiary students' view on information and communications technology usage in Ghana. *Journal of Information Technology Impact*. 9(2), 81–90.

Aly, N., & Akpovi, J. (2001). Total quality management in California public higher education. *Quality Assurance in Education*, 9(3), 127–131.

Barnaghi, P., & Sheth, A. (2014). The Internet of things: The story so far. Retrieved from http://iot.ieee.org/newsletter/september-2014/the-internet-of-things-the-story-so-far.html.

Fuchs, T., & Woessmann, I. (2004). *Computers and Student Learning: Bivariate and Multivariate Evidence on the Availability and Use of Computers at Home and at School*. CESifo Working Paper. No. 1321, November. Munich: Munich Society for the Promotion of Economic Research-CESifo.

Goel, V. P. (2015). Technical and vocational education and training (tvet) system in India for sustainable development. Retrieved from www.unevoc.unesco.org/up/India_Country_Paper.pdf.

Ibrahim, A. T. (2014). Enhancing ICT in Nigerian higher education institutions: Issues and insight. *Open Science Journal of Education*, 2(3), 26–32.

Jattan, De., & Chaudhary, S. (2015). Adoption of ICT in higher education: A study of students' perception towards ICT. *International Journal of Research in Management, Science & Technology*, 3(2), 191–195.

John, S. P. (2015). The integration of information technology in higher education: A study of faculty's attitude towards IT adoption in the teaching process. *Contaduría y Administración*, 60(S1), 230–252.

Kirschner, P., & Woperies, I. G. J. H. (2003). Mindstools for teacher communities. A European perspective. *Technology, Pedagogy and Education*, 12(1), 127–149. Retrieved from www.openscienceonline.com.

Lopez, V. (2003). An exploration of the use of information technologies in the college classroom. *College Quarterly*, 6(1), 1–6. Retrieved from www.college-quarterly.ca/2003-vol. 06-num01 fall/lopes.html.

Mangin, J. P. L. (2011). Modeling perceived usefulness on adopting on line banking through the Tam Model in a Canadian banking environment. *Journal of Internet Banking and Commerce*, 16(1), 13.

Mashhadia, V. Z., & Kargozari, M. R. (2011). Influences of digital classrooms on education. *Procedia Computer Science*, 3, 1178–1183.

Mondal, A., & Mete, J. (2012). ICT in higher education: Opportunities and challenges. Retrieved from http://bcjms.bhattercollege.ac.in/ict-in-higher-education-opportunities-and-challenges.

Roblyer, M. D. (2006). *Integrating Educational Technology into Teaching* (4th Edn). New Jersey: Prentice Hall.

Soloway, E., & Pryor, A. (1996). The next generation in human computer interaction. *Communications of ACM*, 39(4), 16–18.

Sosin, K., Blecha, B. J., Agawal, R., Bartlett, R. I., & Daniel, J. I. (2004). Efficiency in the use of technology in economic education: Some preliminary results. *American Economic Review* (Papers and Proceedings), 34(May), 253–258.

Tsinidou, M., Gerogiannis, V., & Fitsilis, P. (2010). Evaluation of the factors that determine quality in higher education: An empirical study. *Quality Assurance in Education*, 18(3), 227–244.

Wilson, K. B., Tete-Mensah, I., & Boateng, K. A. (2014). Information and communication technology use in higher education: Perspectives from students. *European Scientific Journal*, 10(19), 161–171.

Young, J. (2002). The 24-hour professor. *The Chronicle of Higher Education*, 48(38), 31–33.

Youssef, A. B., & Dahmani, M. (2008). The impact of ICT on student performance in higher education: Direct effects, indirect effects and organisational change. *Revista de Universidad y Sociedad del Conocimiento*, 5(1). Retrieved from www.uoc.edu/rusc/5/1/dt/eng/benyoussef_dahmani.pdf.

Yusuf M. O., & Onasany, S. A. (2004). Information and communication technology ICT and technology in tertiary institution. In E. A. Ogunsakin (Ed.), *Teaching in Tertiary Institutions* (pp. 67–76). Kwara State: University of Ilorin.

5 Analysis of motivational factors using extended TAM approach

Introduction

For the last two decades, Indian HEIs have adopted Information Communication Technologies (ICT) meticulously. Computational technologies and web-based applications offer innovative methods of learning and teaching techniques that makes the learning process considerably more rapid and better. HEIs, particularly universities across the globe, are required to adapt to this rapid change and they need to adopt these new trendy learning technologies so that they can compete with others. This continuous evolution in digital technologies envisages HEIs adopting these trends and paving the way to transform society into a 'knowledge society'. These digital technologies have put new demands on HEIs, with far-reaching implications for their teaching and research functions (Selwyn, 2003; Abu-Shanab & Ababneh, 2015; Lal & Paul, 2018).

Application of digital technologies in education refers to the use of computers and other information and communication tools by all stake holders, i.e. faculty members, students, researchers, information/knowledge managers, etc., for educational purposes that can significantly enhance the quality of learning and education. Some examples of use of digital technologies are: to generate course materials through word processing, Massive Open Online Courses (MOOCs), Computer Assisted Teaching, NET-enabled teaching, e-mail, blogs, etc. Information systems are also used to manage various courses such as Course Management Systems that are increasingly used at the tertiary level. Teachers at the university level may use digital technologies for lesson planning, recording and presenting classes online etc. Another application of new technologies in higher education is to make the course contents available online. The HEIs substantially invest in latest technologies to provide these for their teachers; in return they expect their faculty members to be prepared and motivated in teaching in technology-rich environments (Mangin et al., 2011; John, 2015).

With widespread availability of digital technologies, the academicians are expected to adopt and use these optimally. The acceptance and use of these technologies involve use of computers and other electronic devices such as smart phones and other related items used for teaching and research purposes. This chapter focuses on the teaching community's perception regarding benefits of educational technologies. It is an extension of the Technology Acceptance Model (TAM) devised by Davis in 1989, which is a valuable instrument in predicting individual acceptance and using intentions of online learning technologies. The adoption of these tools depends on self-motivated individuals to make it an effective way of learning.

Review of literature

Some of the previous studies (Roblyer, 2006; Ball & Levy, 2008) demarcate ICT usage in education as the processes and tools involved in addressing the educational needs and problems by using computers and other related electronic resources and technologies. On the other hand, (Bernard & Abrami, 2004; Kingsley, 2007) referred to the applications of IT in education as educational technologies. IT applications in these studies include online LMS, wireless connectivity, high-speed communication infrastructure, accessing course materials through Internet resources, emerging technologies for visual presentation, etc. A study by Bernard and Abrami (2004) argued that usage of educational technologies has increased recently with the use of collaborative learning among faculties and students. On the other hand, Butler and Sellbom (2002) have pointed out that unreliability, resistance to use technologies, poor faculty proficiency in technology and lack of institutional support are major challenges towards use of IT in educational environments.

The Theory of Reasoned Action (TRA) is the foundation for the Technology Acceptance Model (TAM) as proposed by Fred D. Davis in 1989, which is the popular theory in technology adoption space rooted from well-known theory in Human Psychology. TRA proposed that an individual's belief would influence their attitude, which in turn influences their intention and this generates their behaviour towards adopting digital technologies (Fishbein & Ajzen, 1975; Ajzen, 1991). Another study by Fathema et al. (2015) concludes that usability, reliability and adaptability of LMS have a positive association towards its perceived ease of usage. Nanayakkara and Whiddett (2005) in their study revealed that the degree of knowledge and skills in online content design and development strongly impacts the decision of academic staff to adopt this technology. The study finds a strong relationship between the IT literacy rate of staff and system acceptance. The faculty with higher IT literacy are more confident in accepting this technology and would adopt the technology from the early stages of its implementation. Kamali (2012) studied 212 faculty members of an art college in the US Midwest and investigated the factors that predicted the successful adoption and implementation of e-learning technologies and concluded that the academic background did not yield significant correlations with the decision to adopt digital technologies but the results show that the decision to adopt e-learning was influenced by faculty's self-confidence in the use of technology.

Many of the prior technology adoption studies found that not all the functions of LMS were used equally by the handlers. Some functions are used more frequently than others (Panda & Mishra, 2007; Holden & Rada, 2011). Holden and Rada (2011) conclude that teachers' technology self-efficacy has effect on teachers' use of technology. Panda and Mishra (2007) in their study found that the significant barriers of e-learning adoption, as perceived by faculty members, are poor Internet access, lack of training, poor institutional policy and instructional design. The authors found that personal interest in using technology, intellectual challenge and sufficient provision for technology infrastructure were the important motivators in e-learning adoption by faculty members. In their study, Weaver et al. (2008) reported that in using LMS resources, system quality is important to both the students and faculty. Park (2009) also found that e-learning self-efficacy and subjective norms play an important role in affecting students' attitude towards e-learning and behavioural intention to use e-learning.

Technology acceptance model

The acceptance of technology usage by any user is based on two constructs namely, perceived ease of use (PEOU) and perceived usefulness (PU). The original TAM model was conceived and used by Davis (1989). The PU refers to the perceived effectiveness of improving any user's performance, while PEOU refers to how effortless a user perceives using the technology to be. Davis argues that PEOU mostly influences attitude and intention indirectly through PU. Perceived usefulness and user attitude in turn influence intention to use, which predicts actual usage of technology. The original TAM model is depicted in Figure 5.1.

In this study, four variables, namely, motivational factors, encouragement by management, knowledge enhancement opportunities and age are included. They are expected to influence intensity of ICT usage by the faculty members of the sample universities. The analytical framework is depicted in Figure 5.1. Two motivational factors, i.e. self-motivation and

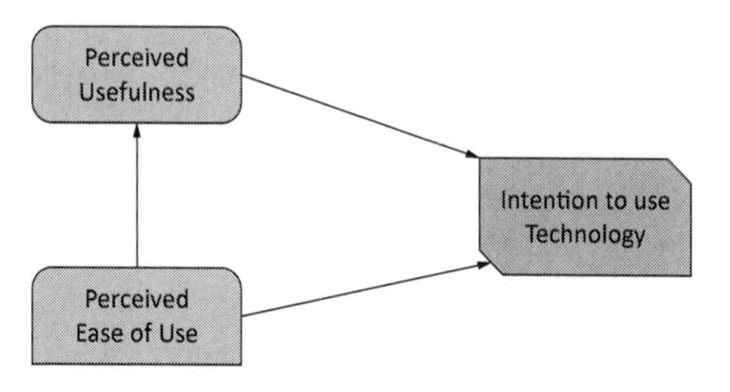

Figure 5.1 Original technology acceptance model.

ease of explaining concepts in the class, are expected to influence adoption of ICT by teachers. The subject streams, management and engineering are ones that need a lot of illustrations, which is easier to explain with help of digital tools, and this could be another factor in adopting NET by faculty.

There is a lot of competition among the HEIs in particular the self-financed universities, to acquire and make use of the latest software technologies. So these institutions are expected to provide incentives such as faculty development initiatives to encourage their teachers to use the available technology to the fullest. As far as the knowledge enhancement opportunities are concerned, learning by doing is probably the way teachers upgrade themselves. Almost all the software and hardware these days have accompanying manuals and online help, which supports the users to learn these on their own to keep themselves abreast of the new technologies. The last variable, i.e. age, is also expected to influence use of digital technologies as younger teachers are more technology savvy and use new technologies more than older faculty members.

Objectives and hypotheses

The availability of digital technologies is pervasive in India as the usage of such technologies makes the learning process immensely active, interesting and enjoyable. Also the service, quality, price and speed are believed to be the main constructs that define the shape of the digital learning phenomenon. Various earlier studies have investigated the acceptance of educational technologies by academicians and students (Wu & Gao, 2011; Lal & Paul, 2015 and others). The study by Wu and Gao (2011) on students' perception of adoption of these technologies found that cognitive factors influence students' perceptions and attitudes towards using educational technology. Another paper by Abu-Shanab and Ababneh (2015) found that age and job satisfaction did not impact adoption of technologies by faculty members of Yarmouk University, Jordan. While earlier studies were based on other aspects that influence the adoption of technology, the present chapter focuses on motivating factors, encouragement by management and other factors influencing the acceptance of digital technologies in the sample universities. The main objectives of the study are:

1 To investigate the factors that motivate the acceptance of NET.
2 To examine whether age has any role to play in NET adoption.
3 To find the role of management in promoting faculty to adopt latest teaching tools.

Based on the objectives, some of the research questions of the study are:

1 To what extent do various motivating factors influence the adoption of digital technologies by faculty in HEIs?
2 In what ways can management encourage faculty to adopt new teaching technologies?

Hypotheses

Davis (1989) argued in his TAM model that any individual's intentions to accept and use any technology is influenced by two variables, namely perceived usefulness and perceived ease of use. The perceived usefulness implies that the user considers the use of technology will improve his/her performance, while perceived ease of use refers to the belief that using the technology will not take too much effort. Based on the above theory, many studies have been undertaken. One of these studies by Cheolho and Sanghoon (2007) investigated the adoption of a wireless Local Area Network (LAN) environment in a discussion-oriented online course study using four variables – perceived usefulness, perceived ease of use, behavioural intention and perceived convenience. They indicated that perceived ease of use had a positive impact on perceived convenience. In another study, Poole (2000) found that students participated in online discussions at a time and place most convenient to them.

Drawing on the theoretical basis of TAM, this chapter takes into account four variables – encouragement by management, motivational factors, knowledge enhancement opportunities and age, to find their influence on NET adoption in Indian universities. It has been argued that the motivating factors such as ease of explaining concepts and self-motivation could influence perceived usefulness of technology adoption. The faculty belonging to management and engineering streams may find digital technologies very convenient in classrooms, more so than the traditional way of teaching. Another reason for using digital technologies could be the initiatives undertaken by the management of the institution. There could be some promotion or financial incentive to adopt ICT for teaching or research. The other variables of study are the age and knowledge enhancement methods by the faculty. Keeping in mind this background of TAM, the following hypotheses are drawn:

H1: Ease of explaining concepts to students positively influences NET adoption

H2: Learning by doing method of knowledge acquisition has a positive impact on intensity of technology use

H3: Faculty development initiatives significantly influences NET adoption

H4: Younger faculty is expected to intensively use digital technologies

H5: Encouragement by management is expected to influence degree of technology use by the faculty members

Sample characteristics

The study in this chapter is based on 43 faculty members in seven HEIs. A semi-structured questionnaire was used to collect data consisting of different variables that capture the attitude of faculty members towards adopting various technology tools. This study is an extension of the robust Technology Acceptance Model (TAM). To check the reliability of the model, Cronbach's alpha was used. Other analytical techniques such as univariate and multivariate analyses were also applied.

The study involved the testing of an extended TAM model on the intensity of NET use for teaching by the faculty members of these seven universities. Apart from personal information of the teaching faculty, details of their intensity of technology adoption, promotion of digital tools by the management and other factors were collected. Four different modes of teaching were included in the study. First, the traditional mode, i.e. using blackboards and whiteboards for teaching; second, the standalone mode, where the teaching involved both traditional and offline modes of computer systems; the third factor included is the usage of institutional servers or intranet along with the first two modes; and the fourth factor involved teaching through Internet apart from other modes.

The study included factors that motivate the faculty to use NET for teaching. The answers were sought on a 5-point scale with 1 as 'least important' and 5 as 'most important'. The different factors included in the study were: self-motivation; management made compulsory; expectations of students; ease of explaining the concepts in class; following other colleagues; encouragement from management; and ease of managing lecture notes. The next query was the method of knowledge enhancement by the teachers in these universities. The faculty were expected to rank their choices on a 5-point scale with 1 'least important' and 5 'most important'. There were four methods of knowledge enhancement included in the study, namely: learning by doing; training is/was organized by the institution; undertaken professional courses; and undertaken subject-specific training. This study also included the role of management in promoting NET use as it is considered an essential aspect. In order to do so, three reasons were used in the analysis, i.e. faculty development initiatives; financial incentives provided; and better job promotion. All the factors were expected to be ranked on the same 5-point scale.

The gender distribution of faculty members shows that females were hired more (55.8 per cent females) than male teachers (44.2 per cent males). This could be due to various reasons. A higher number of female teachers are appointed in self-financed institutions, which has influenced the overall distribution. The preference of women over males could be due to the fact that women prefer teaching jobs to other kind of employment. On the other hand, male teachers switch jobs quite frequently for monetary gains. As a result of this, males are usually not preferred by self-financed institutions.

The distribution of teachers according to their age group shows that majority (44.2 per cent) belonged to the 30–44 age group, while 30.2 per cent belonged to the 45+ age group. Faculty members belonging to the <30 age group represented 25.6 per cent. Efforts were made to draw a representative sample of teachers among all the study streams across universities. The distribution of faculty members according to subject stream indicates that the majority (37.2 per cent) belonged to the management stream. Among the others, 23.3 per cent belonged to social sciences, while 18.6 per cent belonged to the science and engineering stream.

Almost all the universities have technology infrastructure. In response to the multi-response query on the intensity of NET used by the faculty, the majority (74.4 per cent) replied that they used intranet, 27.9 per cent of faculty members reported that they used the traditional mode, 46.5 per cent used standalone and 32.6 per cent used the Internet for teaching purposes.

The sample universities in the study were categorized according to their source of funding. The government-funded institutions that have been in existence for a long time are termed public, namely: University of Delhi, Jawaharlal Nehru University and Jamia Millia Islamia University. The public-funded university, which came into existence after year 2000, is categorized as 'public-new', i.e. Gautam Buddha University. The need to categorize public and public-new is due to the fact that the infrastructure and human resources are very different in these institutions. The public-new institution is equipped with state-of-the-art technology and the faculty is young and motivated, while in public universities this is not the case. The remaining universities, namely, Ansal University, Northcap University and Symbiosis International University, are categorized as private. Across all the institutions, 43 teachers in total were interviewed. The analysis of their opinions on various aspects of NET is presented in this section. Figure 5.2 depicts the gender distribution of teachers. The details of the data related to Figures 5.2 to 5.13 are presented in Appendix 5.1.

It can be seen from Figure 5.2 that male teachers are in the majority in public institutions (68.8 per cent), while females prefer private institutions (78.9 per cent). This may be due to various reasons. One of them could be that the mobility of female teachers is controlled by their social settings, as they prefer to take employment near their location of stay. On the other hand, male teachers switch jobs quite frequently for monetary gains.

The distribution of teachers according to their age is depicted in Figure 5.3.

It can be seen from Figure 5.3 that the teachers in public universities in the highest age bracket, i.e. 45+ years, is 56.3 per cent. The age-wise distribution of teachers is quite obvious. The new institutions, whether private or public, are expected to employ young faculty, while in the older institutions, the average age of faculty is supposed to be higher. This is substantiated by the fact that 78.9 per cent of the teachers in private universities and 100 per cent of teachers in public-new institutions are below the age of 45 years. Hence the association is statistically significant at the level of 1 per cent.

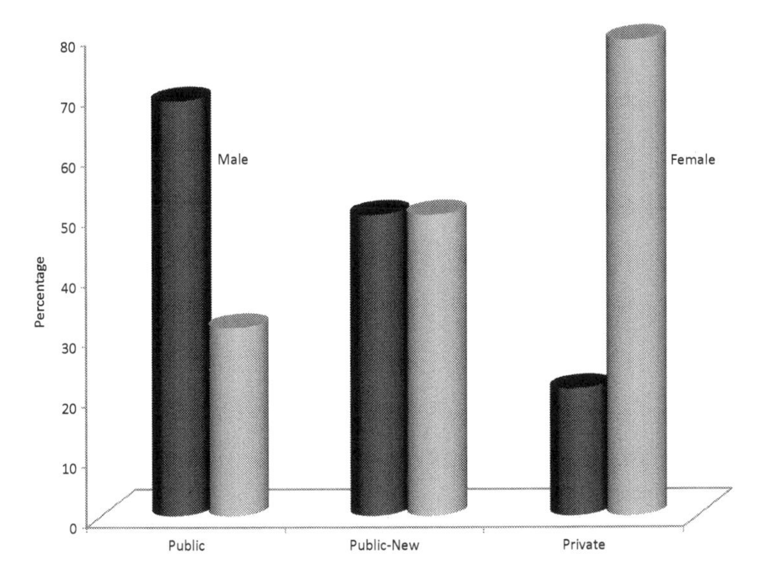

Figure 5.2 Gender distribution of teachers.

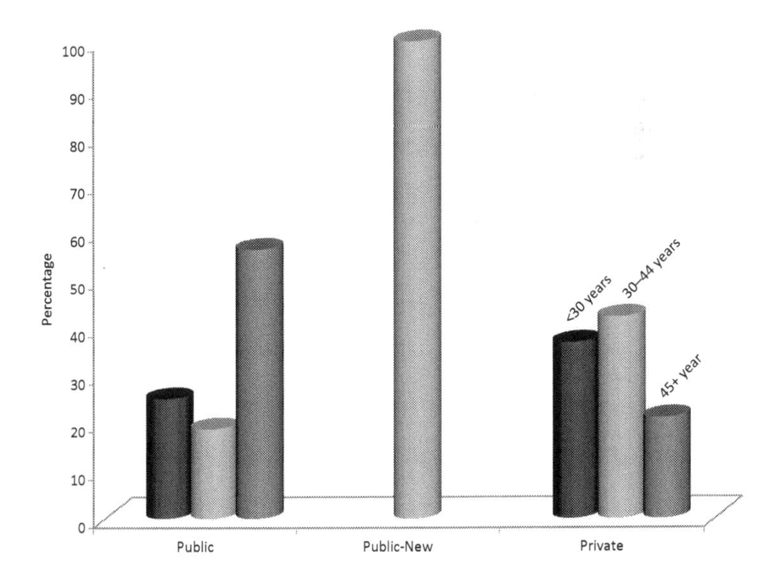

Figure 5.3 Distribution of teachers by age.

The stream-wise distribution of the faculty members is presented in Figure 5.4.

Efforts were made to draw a representative sample from teachers of all the streams across the universities. The distribution presented in Figure 5.4 shows that the teachers in public universities are from traditional courses. This is because the public universities focus on traditional courses and hence the sample of teachers is drawn from sciences and social sciences faculty. On the other hand, the focus of public-new universities is on modern courses, i.e. engineering and management. Hence the sample is limited to engineering and management courses. The private universities have to take care of both traditional and new courses. Hence a representative sample is drawn from all the streams.

Figure 5.5 depicts whether the university campus is Wi-Fi enabled. It is worth mentioning here that most of the departments within the public-funded universities had some Wi-Fi-enabled departments rather than the university as a whole.

Although the majority of teachers (75 per cent) replied in the negative with regards to the availability of Wi-Fi in public universities, it was found during the survey that several individual departments had access to these technologies. Another reason for non-availability of Wi-Fi in the entire campus is due to the sprawling structure of the public university campuses.

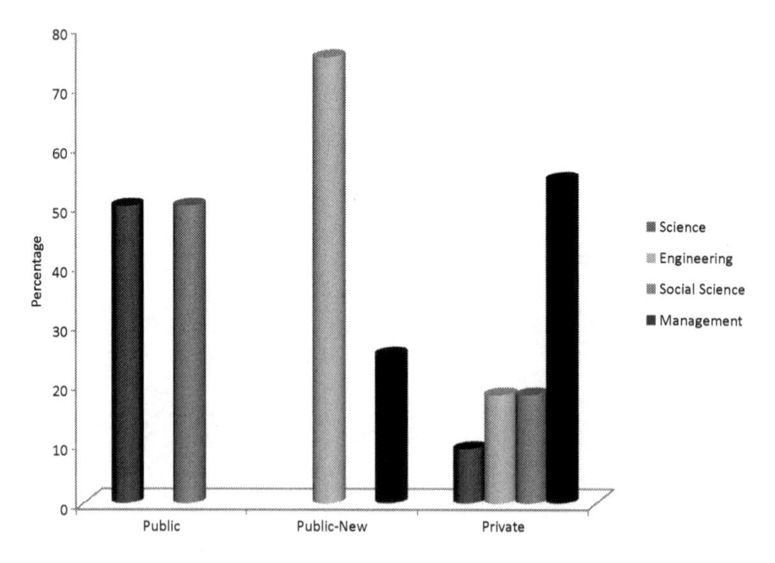

Figure 5.4 Distribution of teachers by stream.

On the other hand, the campuses of recently established institutions are quite compact and new networking technologies can be provided with comparatively less financial resources.

The response on the various modes of teaching adopted by the faculty members is indicated in Figure 5.6. This is a multi-response question as more than one modes of teaching could be adopted by the faculty.

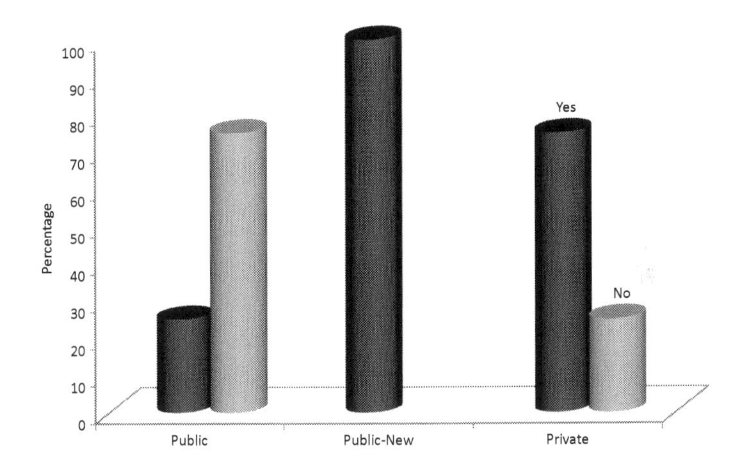

Figure 5.5 Wi-Fi enabled campus.

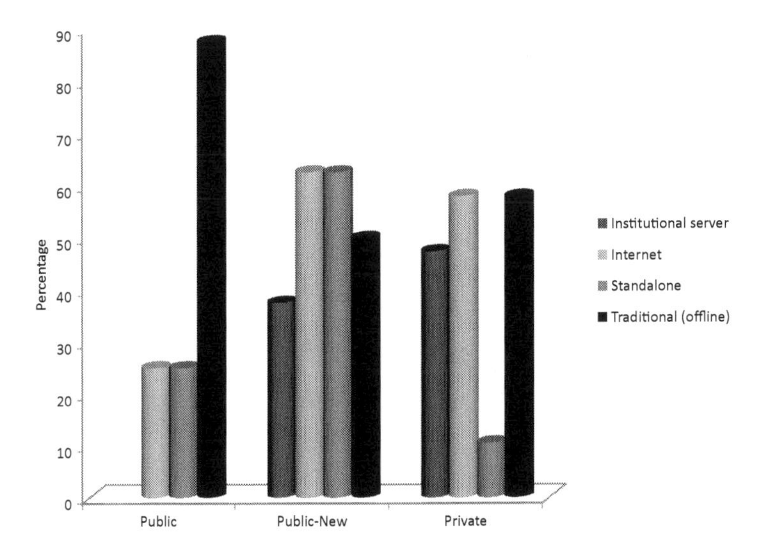

Figure 5.6 Mode of teaching.

Figure 5.6 shows that the most preferred mode of teaching is using an institutional server (47.4 per cent) and the Internet (57.9 per cent) in private institutions. It can also be seen from the figure that a substantially large percentage of faculty in all the institutions preferred the traditional mode of teaching. This may be due to preferred choice of students. In the case of public-new institutions, the most preferred modes are Internet and standalone (62.5 per cent each). The faculty in public institutions, on the other hand, prefer the offline mode (87.5 per cent) followed by standalone and Internet (25.0 per cent each). It may be inferred from the results that newer teaching technologies are preferred in new institutions, though traditional modes of teaching are still the preferred choice by a large percentage of teachers in all the institutions.

The result of another multi-response question regarding classroom equipment is depicted in Figure 5.7.

Figure 5.7 also indicates that, in privately owned institutions, the majority of teachers opined that classrooms are equipped with whiteboards (94.7 per cent) followed by computers with Internet access (63.2 per cent). In the case of public-new institutions, all the teachers indicated that the classrooms are equipped with whiteboards while 75.0 per cent reported that Internet accessibility is also available. A similar trend is visible in public universities, with 56.3 per cent of the teachers using a whiteboard, and 43.8 per cent indicating the availability of Internet access. The figure

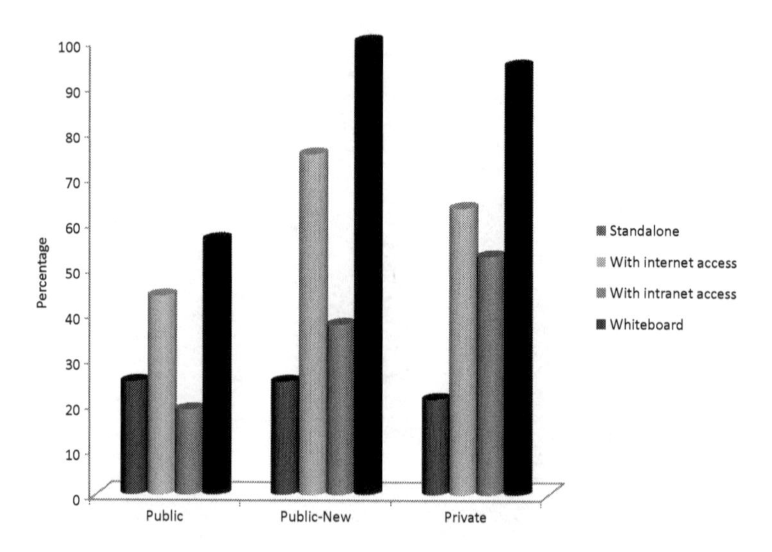

Figure 5.7 Classroom equipment.

shows that a fairly large percentage of faculty across the institutions opined that classrooms are equipped with whiteboards, suggesting that these are used effectively. The results substantiate the earlier findings that the preferred mode of teaching is still traditional. It may be inferred from the results that classrooms in public-new and private institutions are equipped with traditional as well as modern technologies, while classrooms in public-funded universities are equipped with whiteboards and are not well equipped with modern teaching tools.

The opinion on the motivational factors for using NET in teaching was also sought. The opinions were collected on a 5-point Likert scale, i.e. 1 'least imp.' 2 'less imp.' 3 'to some extent', 4 'important', 5 'most important'. The average of the opinions thus collected were computed and presented in Figure 5.8.

It can be seen from Figure 5.8 that 'self-motivation' received the highest score of 4.50, 4.76 and 4.48 in public, public-new, and private universities respectively, suggesting that self-motivation is considered the most important factor in the adoption of NET for teaching. The second motivating factor in public universities is 'ease of managing lecture notes', while 'ease of explaining concepts' has taken second place in public-new and private universities. Although faculty members in private institutions have not reported this, there could be some pressure from management to adopt digital technologies in teaching in these institutions. The expectation

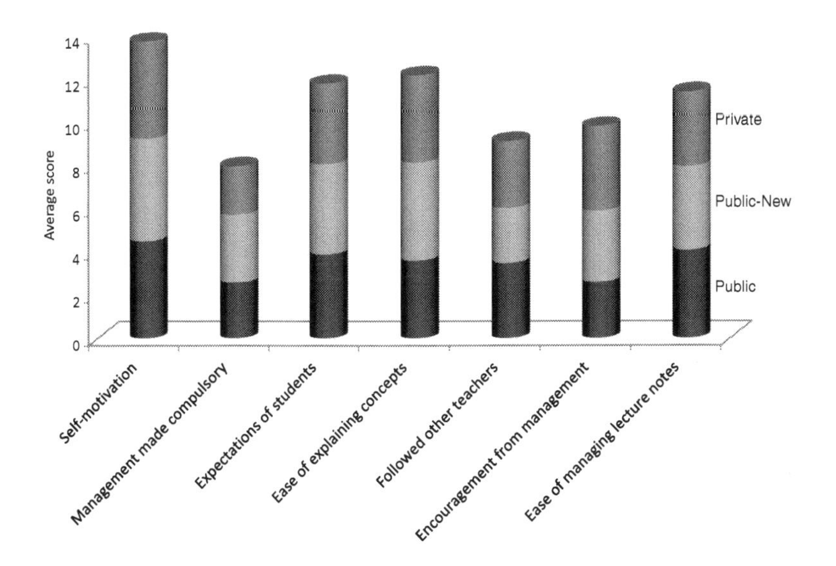

Figure 5.8 Motivational factors.

of students also received a high score in all types of institutions. It is clear from the results that self-motivation and expectation of students are the main factors in the adoption of new technologies irrespective of the funding nature of the institution. The results are as expected.

It was thought necessary to evaluate the function-specific use of new technologies by the faculty. In this context, teachers were requested to give their opinion on frequency of use of digital technologies. The responses were sought on a 5-point Likert scale, i.e. 1 'rarely', 2 'several times a month', 3 'once a week', 4 'twice a week', 5 'Everyday'. The average opinions are presented in Figure 5.9.

Figure 5.9 shows that the average scores (more than 4) given by the faculty members of all the institutions for 'browse/search Internet' is highest among all other tools. It may be inferred that faculty members of all the institutions browse the Internet almost on a daily basis. The teachers at public-new institutions assigned a similar rank (4.39) to 'prepare digital lectures on standalone system'. The other tools that were used twice a week (average rank around 4) are 'communicate online with management', 'prepare digital exercises and tasks for students' and 'look for online professional development opportunities', while faculty members of private institutions used these tools once a week (average rank around 3). The teachers at public institutions 'look for online professional development opportunities' once a week (average score 3.20). It may be inferred from the analysis that the faculty members of public-new and private institutions use digital technologies, except Internet browsing, more frequently than faculty at public-funded institutions.

The next query pertains to the acquisition and upgradation of knowledge about new teaching technologies. Opinions were sought on a 5-point

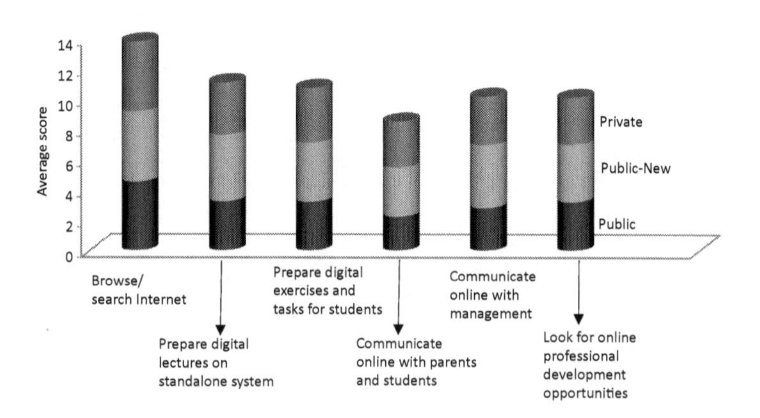

Figure 5.9 Digital technology tools used and their purposes.

Likert scale, i.e. 1 'least imp.', 2 'less imp.', 3 'to some extent', 4 'important', 5 'most important'. Based on their ranking, average scores were computed and are presented in Figure 5.10.

It can be seen from the figure that the teachers at all the institutions chose 'learning by doing' as their most preferred (average score of more than 4) way of upgrading their ability to use digital technologies. The second choice as rated by the teachers is taking subject-specific training. The opinion of all the teachers is similar irrespective of the nature of institution on the modes of skill upgradation.

It was considered important to ascertain the views of teachers on the promotion of NET use by the management. There could be several incentives to do this, such as faculty development, financial and job promotion. In this context, the faculty members were requested to rank their choices on a 5-point Likert scale, i.e. 1 'least imp.', 2 'less imp.', 3 'to some extent', 4 'important', 5 'most important'. Figure 5.11 presents the average scores.

It seems that management has very little role to play in the promotion of use of digital technologies in public-funded universities. To some extent this is very obvious, as the management in such institutions do not have much say in the financial and job promotion opportunities of faculty members. The opinion expressed by the teachers of public-funded institutions substantiate this point as the average opinion is around 3. The faculty members of private and public-new institutions opined that 'faculty development initiatives' by management are most important and are actively undertaken by them. Another distinguishing characteristic between public and private institutions

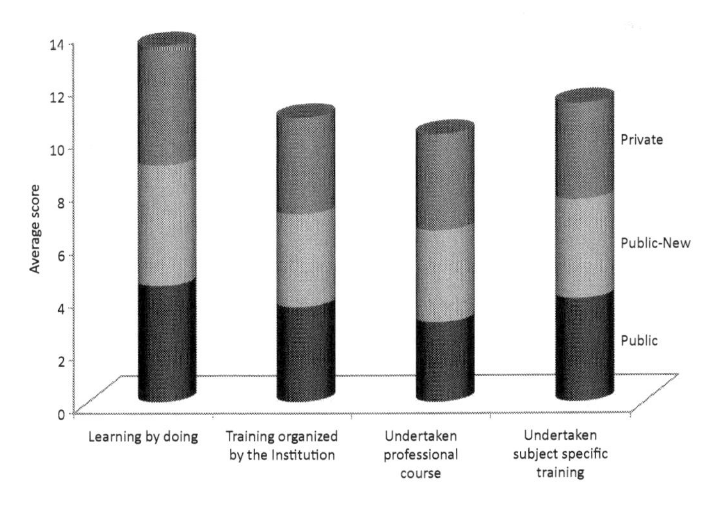

Figure 5.10 Upgradation and acquisition of ICT skills.

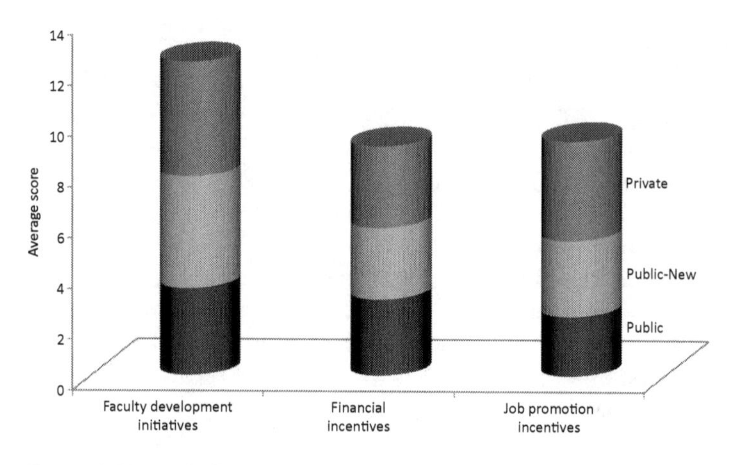

Figure 5.11 Promotion of ICT use by management.

is that job promotion incentives are considered important in the promotion of NET use in public-new and private institutions, with an average score of 3.00 and 3.91 respectively. This is also as expected as the management at private institutions do not have to follow a rigid promotion policy.

The rate of obsolescence of digital technologies is very high and hence they need to be upgraded frequently in order to remain up to date. This might be difficult for public-funded institutions as they would need a regular grant in order to do this. In this context, the opinion of the institutions on the sustainability of these initiatives was sought. Out of a total of 43 respondents, 27 responded positively while 4 responded negatively. The remaining 12 did not respond. Of the 27 respondents who were positive about it, the percentage of teachers in public, public-new and private institutions were 29.7, 22.2 and 48.1 respectively. The results show that almost a quarter of respondents in public and public-new institutions were sure about the sustainability of the existing NET infrastructure, while nearly half of the faculty members in private institutions shared the same views.

The literature on NET diffusion in higher education in developing countries suggests that there could be many obstacles, such as irrelevance of such technologies, lack of familiarity, lack of initiatives and lack of appreciation, by management, students etc. Hence it was considered important to identify the obstacles in diffusion of NET in the Indian context. The opinions of teachers on various obstacles were sought on a 5-point Likert scale, i.e. 1 'least imp.', 2 'less imp.', 3 'to some extent', 4 'important', 5 'most important'. The average scores are presented in Figure 5.12.

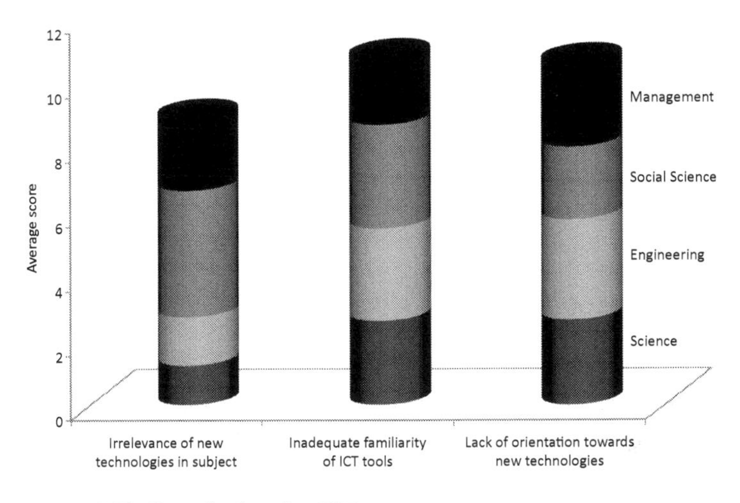

Figure 5.12 Obstacles in using ICT.

The obstacles included in Figure 5.12 are not institution-specific. Therefore the analysis is performed subject-wise. Although, looking at the rankings given by the faculty members from across the streams, none of the above are considered an obstacle in NET use except in social science. Social science teachers felt that too much of NET is not very relevant for their stream. Sciencc, engineering and management teachers ranked all the options as less or least important, thereby suggesting that these are not obstacles at all in their use of digital technologies.

Repondents' opinions were sought on institutional obstacles in using digital technologies. Their opinions were again sought on a 5-point Likert scale, i.e. 1 'least imp.', 2 'less imp.', 3 'to some extent', 4 'important', 5 'most important'. Figure 5.13 presents an analysis of the opinions.

It can be seen from Figure 5.13 that all the institutional obstacles were ranked around 3 by the faculty members of all the universities, thereby suggesting that these are only considered to be obstacles to some extent. Among the options, 'inappropriate ICT infrastructure in the institution' is considered an obstacle to some extent by public institutions, whereas the teachers of public-new and private institutions considered it less important. It may be inferred that by and large faculty members in all the institutions opined that there are no major obstacles in the adoption of digital technologies.

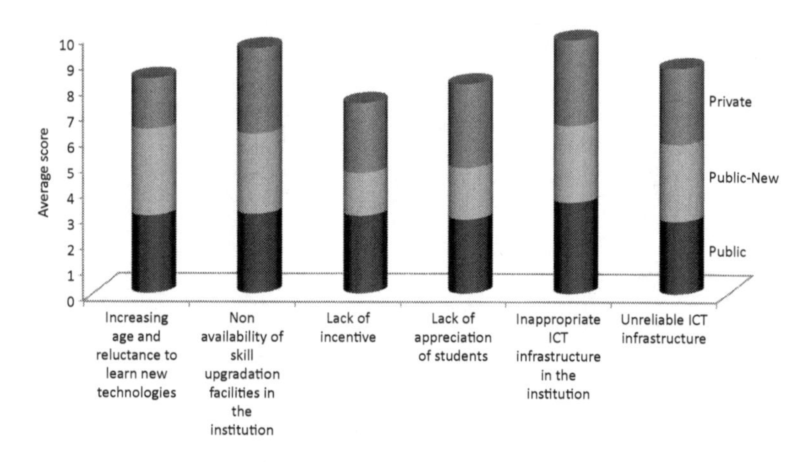

Figure 5.13 Institutional obstacles in using ICT.

TAM analysis

The data have been subjected to a reliability test to determine the internal consistency of items under study. Cronbach's alpha is used to measure the internal consistency, i.e. to establish how closely related a set of items are as a group. The best fit or preferred value of the test is when the alpha value is between 0.80 and 0.90. It is considered to be a measure of scale reliability. The value of Cronbach's alpha for five constructs in this study is almost 0.7 (0.677). Thus the result indicates that the questionnaire is a reliable measurement instrument.

Subsequently the data are subjected to Ordered Probit analysis, as the dependent variable is ordinal in nature. The results are depicted in Figure 5.14.

The results show that one of the motivating factors (ease of explaining the concepts in class) highly influences the adoption of NET by the faculty members. This could be due to the fact that the teachers of management, science and engineering streams are more inclined towards using digital technologies for their teaching and research activities. The result is statistically significant at 5 per cent. The knowledge enhancement factor, i.e. learning by doing, also significantly influences intensity of technology use (significance level of 5 per cent). Thus the first and second hypotheses holds true.

The management of self-financed universities in particular invest heavily in digital infrastructure for the faculty members and students. They devise incentives in order to encourage teachers to use these tools intensively. Thus

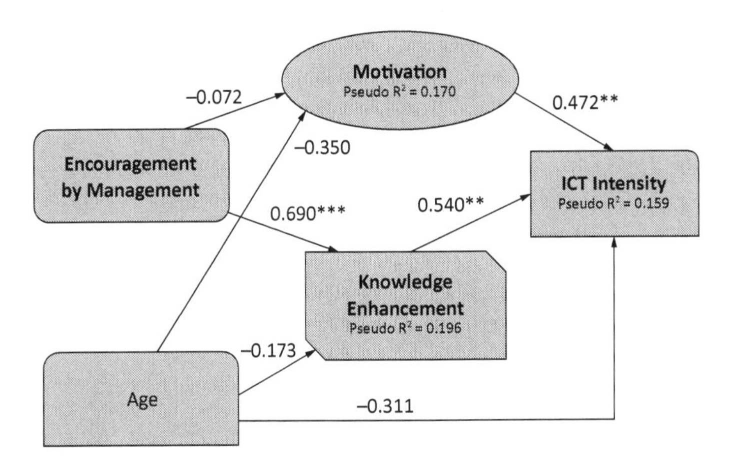

Figure 5.14 Extended TAM model.

the role of management is important in NET adoption, which is reflected by a highly significant (1 per cent) association between management's role and knowledge enhancement. There could be various methods of knowledge enhancement of the teachers such as faculty development initiatives.

The association between age of the faculty members and the motivating factor (ease of explaining the concepts in class) is negative and insignificant. The findings are quite noticeable as younger faculty are not only technology savvy but are also expected to be concerned about this motivational factor, keeping in mind their future career. While for the senior faculty, future career is not very important, hence they may not be very concerned about this motivational factor and therefore assigned it a low importance.

Irrespective of the financial nature of the institution, the faculty members are involved in acquisition and enhancement of knowledge regarding digital tools. Figure 5.14 shows that the faculty development initiatives are encouraged by the management, which in turn influences their knowledge enhancement. The result is highly significant at 1 per cent. Thus, the fifth hypothesis, i.e. knowledge enhancement activities are encouraged by management, holds true.

Summary and conclusions

This chapter aimed to identify the factors that influence the adoption of digital technologies in Indian HEIs. The conceptual framework used in the study was the extended Technology Acceptance Model (TAM). The study focused on the teaching community's perception regarding the benefits of educational technologies. An extended TAM was used to predict teachers' acceptance and usage intentions of online learning technologies.

In order to check the reliability of the model, Cronbach's alpha was used. Subsequently, Ordered Probit analysis was applied for robustness of results. The value of Cronbach's alpha for five constructs in this study was almost 0.7 (0.677), which is an acceptable value. The study found that one of the motivating factors (i.e. ease of explaining the concepts in class) highly influences the adoption of digital technologies by the faculty members. This could be due to the fact that the teachers of management, science and engineering streams are more inclined towards using new technologies for their teaching activities. The result is statistically significant at 5 per cent. The knowledge enhancement factor, i.e. learning by doing, also significantly influenced the intensity of NET use (significance level of 5 per cent). The study also established the importance of institutional support, particularly in the role of management, in encouraging the teachers' towards using these digital technologies. The results show significant association between role of management in encouragement of new technology use and adoption of knowledge enhancement activities.

Appendix 5.1: faculty data analysis

Table 5.A1 Gender distribution of teachers

University type → Gender	*Public*	*Public-new*	*Private*	*Total*
Male	11 (68.8)	4 (50.0)	4 (21.1)	19 (44.2)
Female	5 (31.2)	4 (50.0)	15 (78.9)	24 (55.8)
Total	16 [37.2]	8 [18.6]	19 [31.4]	43 [100.0]

Note
Chi-square = 8.147; Sig. = 0.017: Figures in parentheses are column %; square brackets are row %.

Table 5.A2 Distribution of teachers by age

University type → Age	*Public*	*Public-new*	*Private*	*Total*
<30 years	4 (25.0)	–	7 (36.8)	11 (25.6)
30–44	3 (18.7)	8 (100.0)	8 (42.1)	19 (44.2)
45+	9 (56.3)	–	4 (21.1)	13 (30.2)
Total	16 [37.2]	8 [18.6]	19 [31.4]	43 [100.0]

Note
Chi-square = 17.523; Sig. = 0.0023: Figures in parentheses are column %; square brackets are row %.

Table 5.A3 Distribution of teachers by stream

University type → Stream	*Public*	*Public-new*	*Private*	*Total*
Science	8 (50.0)	–	1 (9.1)	9 (20.9)
Engineering	–	6 (75.0)	2 (18.2)	8 (18.6)
Social Science	8 (50.0)	–	2 (18.2)	10 (23.3)
Management	–	2 (25.0)	14 (54.5)	16 (37.2)
Total	16 [35.7]	8 [19.0]	19 [45.2]	43 [100.0]

Note
Chi-square = 47.352; Sig. = 0.000: Figures in parentheses are column %; square brackets are row %.

Table 5.A4 Wi-Fi enabled campus

University type → Responses	*Public*	*Public-new*	*Private*	*Total*
Yes	4 (25.0)	8 (100.0)	16 (75.0)	28 (65.1)
No	12 (75.0)	–	3 (25.0)	15 (34.9)
Total	16 [37.2]	8 [18.6]	19 [31.4]	43 [100.0]

Note
Chi-square = 18.6715; Sig. = 0.000: Figures in parentheses are column %; square brackets are row %.

Table 5.A5 Mode of teaching

University type → Responses	*Public*	*Public-new*	*Private*	*Total*
Institutional server	–	3 (37.5)	9 (47.4)	12 [27.9]
Internet	4 (25.0)	5 (62.5)	11 (57.9)	20 [46.5]
Standalone	4 (25.0)	5 (62.5)	2 (10.5)	10 [25.6]
Traditional (offline)	14 (87.5)	4 (50.0)	11 (57.9)	29 [67.4]

Note
Figures in parentheses are percentage of total respondents in each category of institution; square brackets are percentage of total respondents.

Table 5.A6 Classroom equipment

University type → Equipment	*Public*	*Public-new*	*Private*	*Total*
Standalone	4 (25.0)	2 (25.0)	4 (21.1)	10 [23.3]
With internet access	7 (43.8)	6 (75.0)	12 (63.2)	25 [58.1]
With intranet access	3 (18.8)	3 (37.5)	10 (52.6)	16 [37.2]
Whiteboard	9 (56.3)	8 (100.0)	18 (94.7)	35 [81.4]

Note
Figures in parentheses are percentage of total respondents in each category of institution; square brackets are percentage of total respondents.

Table 5.A7 Motivational factors

University type → Factors	*Public*	*Public-new*	*Private*
Self-motivation	4.50	4.76	4.48
Management made compulsory	2.58	3.15	2.25
Expectations of students	3.89	4.19	3.72
Ease of explaining concepts	3.60	4.55	4.04
Followed other teachers	3.48	2.56	3.11
Encouragement from management	2.60	3.31	3.92
Ease of managing lecture notes	4.08	3.89	3.45

Note
Figures are average scores.

Table 5.A8 Digital technology tools used and their purposes

University type → Activities	*Public*	*Public-new*	*Private*
Browse/search Internet	4.52	4.66	4.61
Prepare digital lectures on standalone system	3.24	4.39	3.47
Prepare digital exercises and tasks for students	3.21	3.93	3.60
Communicate online with parents and students	2.22	3.25	3.05
Communicate online with management	2.79	4.16	3.23
Look for online professional development opportunities	3.20	3.79	3.12

Note
Figures are average scores.

Table 5.A9 Upgradation and acquisition of ICT skills

University type → Choices	*Public*	*Public-new*	*Private*
Learning by doing	4.38	4.56	4.52
Training organized by the institution	3.58	3.50	3.64
Undertaken professional course	3.00	3.45	3.64
Undertaken subject-specific training	3.88	3.75	3.64

Note
Figures are average scores.

Table 5.A10 Promotion of ICT use by management

University type → Choices	*Public*	*Public-new*	*Private*
Faculty development initiatives	3.42	4.41	4.50
Financial incentives	3.00	2.82	3.21
Job promotion incentives	2.33	3.00	3.91

Note
Figures are average scores.

Table 5.A11 Obstacles in using ICT

Subjects → Obstacles	*Science*	*Engineering*	*Social science*	*Management*
Irrelevance of new technologies in subject	1.22	1.50	3.92	2.24
Inadequate familiarity of ICT tools	2.60	2.87	3.21	2.05
Lack of orientation towards new technologies	2.63	3.11	2.25	2.60

Note
Figures are average scores.

Table 5.A12 Institutional obstacles in using ICT

University type → Obstacles	*Public*	*Public-new*	*Private*
Increasing age and reluctance to learn new technologies	3.00	3.38	1.96
Non-availability of skill upgradation facilities in the institution	3.07	3.13	3.31
Lack of incentive	3.00	1.67	2.72
Lack of appreciation of students	2.87	2.00	3.26
Inappropriate ICT infrastructure in the institution	3.53	3.00	3.32
Unreliable ICT infrastructure	2.81	3.00	2.95

Note
Figures are average scores.

References

Abu-Shanab, E., & Ababneh, L. (2015). Exploring academicians acceptance of e-learning using an extended TAM: The case of Yarmouk University. *Journal of Network Communications and Emerging Technologies*, 1(1), 1–5.

Ajzen, I. (1991). The theory of planned behavior. *Organizational Behavior and Human Decision Processes* (50), 179–211.

Ball, D., & Levy, Y. (2008). Emerging educational technology: Assessing the factors that influence instructors' acceptance in information systems and other classrooms. *Journal of Information Systems Education*, 19(4), 431–444.

Bernard, R., & Abrami, P. (2004). How does distance education compare with classroom instruction? A meta-analysis of the empirical literature. *Review of Educational Research*, 74(3), 379–439.

Butler, D. L., & Sellbom, M. (2002). Barriers to adopting technology for teaching and learning. *EDUCAUSE Quarterly*, (November), 22–28.

Cheolho, Y., & Sanghoon, K. (2007). Convenience and TAM in a ubiquitous computing environment: The case of wireless LAN. *Electronic Commerce Research and Applications* 6(1), 102–112.

Davis, F. D. (1989). Perceived usefulness, perceived ease of use, and user acceptance of information technology. *MIS Quarterly*, 13(3), 318–339.

Fathema, N., Shannon, D., & Margaret, R. (2015). Expanding the Technology Acceptance Model (TAM) to examine faculty use of Learning Management Systems (LMSs) in higher education institutions. *MERLOT Journal of Online Learning and Teaching*, 11(2), 210–232.

Fishbein, M., & Ajzen, I. (1975). *Belief, Attitude, Intention, and Behavior: An Introduction to Theory and Research.* Reading, MA: Addison-Wesley Pub. Co.

Holden, H., & Rada, R. (2011). Understanding the influence of perceived usability and technology self-efficacy on teachers' technology acceptance. *Journal of Research on Technology in Education (International Society for Technology in Education)*, 43(4), 343–367.

John, S. P. (2015). The integration of information technology in higher education: A study of faculty's attitude towards IT adoption in the teaching process. *Contaduría y Administración: Accounting and Management*, 60(S1), 230–252.

Kamali, A. (2012). Antecedents of adopting e-learning: Toward a model of academic e-learning acceptance culture. *Proceedings of the Information Systems Educators Conference 2012 New Orleans Louisiana*, Louisiana, USA, 1–9.

Kingsley, K. V. (2007). Empower diverse learners with educational technology and digital media. *Intervention in School and Clinic*, 43(1), 52–56.

Lal, K., & Paul, S. (2015). Quality of teachers and skill formation in students. *Indian Journal of Teacher Education*, 1(1), 85–98.

Lal, K., & Paul, S. (2018). New educational technologies in tertiary education in India: Adoption and consequences. *Journal of Applied Research in Higher Education*, 10(1), 1–14.

Mangin, J. P. L., Bourgault, N., Guerrero, M. M., & Egea, J. M. O. (2011). Modelling perceived usefulness on adopting online banking through the Tam model in a Canadian banking environment. *Journal of Internet Banking and Commerce*, 16(1), 1–23.

Nanayakkara, C., & Whiddett, R. J. (2005). A model of user acceptance of e-learning technologies: A case study of a polytechnic in New Zealand. Retrieved from http://citeseerx.ist.psu.edu/viewdoc/summary?doi=10.1.1.513.7409.

Panda, S., & Mishra, S. (2007). E-learning in a mega open university: Faculty attitude, barriers and motivators. *Educational Media International*, 44(4), 323–338.

Park, S. Y. (2009). An analysis of the Technology Acceptance Model in understanding university students' behavioral intention to use e-learning. *Educational Technology & Society*, 12(3), 150–162.

Poole, D. M. (2000). Student participation in a discussion-oriented online course: A case study. *Journal of Research on Computing in Education*, 33(2), 162–177.

Roblyer, M. D. (2006). *Integrating Educational Technology into Teaching* (4th Edn). Upper Saddle River, NJ: Prentice Hall.

Selwyn, N. (2003). ICT for all? Access and use of public ICT sites in the UK. *Information, Communication & Society*, 6(3), 350–375.

Weaver, D., Spratt, C., & Nair, C. (2008). Academic and student use of a LMS: Implications for quality, *Australasian Journal of Educational Technology*, 24(1), 30–41.

Wu, X., & Gao, Y. (2011). Applying the extended technology acceptance model to the use of clickers in student learning: Some evidence from macroeconomics classes. *American Journal of Business Education*, 4(7), 43–50.

6 Role of management in promotion of NET use

There are three stakeholders in any academic institution, i.e. management, teachers and students. This book includes the views of all stakeholders. The management in these institutions are representative of those responsible for providing NET facilities. Although the views of all stakeholders were collected using a semi-structured instrument, it is not possible to statistically analyse the views of the management. Hence they are presented as qualitative evidence of the availability and use of digital technologies in these institutions. The views of institutions are as follows.

Identification of promotional factors

The potential of NET as a driver and innovator in HEIs is unchallenged. But the potential of this technology, to enrich and enhance the teaching and learning process and to support flexible learning modes, has been realized by the institutions' management. The increasing use of digital technologies in higher education has led to quality enhancements in teaching and learning at all levels of higher education. Universities worldwide are moving from traditional forms of teaching to online and virtual environments. The use of NET in education not only improves classroom teaching and the learning process, but also provides the facility of e-learning. The teaching community is able to reach remote areas and learners are able to access a qualitative learning environment from anywhere and at anytime. It is important that teachers or trainers should be made to adopt technology in their teaching styles in order to provide pedagogical and educational gains for learners. In order to achieve this, the management of HEIs have a greater role to play in successfully implementing these technologies and to empower teachers and support them in acquiring computer skills and obtaining software and equipment. Hence the promotional factors take a pivotal role in diffusion of digital technologies.

Although faculty members could be motivated by several factors, the present study groups them into three main categories, namely: faculty development initiatives; financial incentives and better job promotion; and administrative measures. Initiatives in faculty development initiatives could be taken, such as organizing regular training programmes in the institutions by invited faculty from other institutions, in-house training through online courses such as MOOCs, by inviting professional firms for imparting training, and sending faculty to attend courses organized by other institutions. While financial and better job promotion opportunities are persuasive measures more relevant in private institutions, administrative instruments in public-funded institutions could also be used as a means to promote the use of NET.

Several studies have investigated the role of promotional initiatives. In this context, a study by Johnson et al. (2012) on Carroll University, Waukesha, USA, found that financial instruments were very important. The university, a liberal arts university, has 112 full-time faculty. The management recognized the faculty's unwillingness to learn about online teaching and learning and started to provide faculty development initiatives such as stipends for the teachers. The authors conclude that faculty development initiatives, such as providing additional pay, does help in encouraging teachers and sends a message that the administration is serious about helping the faculty to learn about digital technologies. Another study by Suliman et al. (2008) on four Sudanese universities reveals that a lack of funds is the major barrier in implementing NET in these universities. The management has opined that budgetary constraints have adversely affected staff retention, particularly the academics. The faculty could not be provided sufficient benefits and as a result they were not professionally satisfied and could not be retained. The authors further concluded that Sudan lacks local technology training facilities and manpower, and thus most of their ICT personnel from the government and private sector received their training abroad.

Another study by Valcke (2003) on Ghent University, Flanders (Belgium), regarding campus-wide e-learning approaches, advocates the implementation of a good practices approach wherein the active involvement of teaching staff is ensured and is a reward system for their involvement in higher education innovation. The teaching staff engaged in teaching and learning processes receive a 500 Euro bonus or a digital camera from the management. This proved to be good financial instrument in the promotion of digital technologies.

Public-funded institutions

Jawaharlal Nehru University

The management of JNU opined that use of NET substantially varies from one course to another. For instance, in social science courses the use of NET is very limited, while in science subjects, engineering, and PhD programmes the usage is extensive. It was ascertained that application software was either developed in-house or the university used open source software. There was no compulsion from the university to use a particular type of NET in the classroom, rather the choice lies with the teacher concerned. Regarding the motivational factors of teachers to use NET, the concerned official of the university stated that the initiatives for teachers and students are considered very important. On the question of sustainability of the existing NET infrastructure, the management feels that it is very much sustainable. The faculty is motivated to use NET by sending them to other universities through sabbatical leave or faculty exchange programmes. The university feels that use of NET has attracted more students and more qualified faculty.

Jamia Millia Islamia

As far as the subject-wise usage of NET is concerned, it was very high in engineering, management and PhD programmes, while in other courses the usage was very limited. The decision to use new technologies in the classroom lies with the individual teacher or heads of the departments. There was no compulsion from the higher authorities regarding extent of digital technology usage. As informed by the management, the students preferred either standalone or traditional methods of teaching in the classroom. Although, the management never interfered in the use of new technologies in teaching, the university facilitated provision of such technologies. The initiatives of teachers and students also contributed to the adoption of NET. JMI is the only institution that reported that present NET infrastructure may not be sustainable as there is no provision of regular funding of such activities. The technologies were funded by a one-time grant.

The obsolescence rate of digital technologies is very high. Therefore it is very important that the faculty is regularly updated about the development of teaching technologies. This was achieved by organizing regular training programmes and the participation of teachers in faculty upgradation programmes organized by other institutions. JMI did not have any mechanism to motivate faculty in remaining up to date in teaching methodologies. Unlike private universities, JMI could not offer any financial incentive either. With regard to the impact of adoption of NET, the quality of teaching and research has improved.

Gautam Buddha University

NET is used extensively in engineering and IT-related courses at GBU. The PhD scholars also use new technologies very effectively. The usage is very limited in traditional courses such as BA, BCom, BSc, MA, M.Com and MSc. Surprisingly, usage is also limited in management courses. The institution, being new, has not been able to evolve in-house competencies to develop software for its needs. Hence either open source or proprietary systems are being used. The decision to use new technologies lies with the teachers. The university management does not interfere in such matters. The online mode of teaching is only preferred in engineering courses. Students still prefer to submit projects and assignment offline. The teachers' initiative is considered to be the most important motivating factor in usage of NET. Despite facing serious problems in maintaining existing digital infrastructure, the management is confident that digital technology initiatives are sustainable.

The university encourages the faculty to increase the use of digital technologies in teaching by several means. The faculty is sent to participate in national and international conferences. Initially the faculty was offered professional development allowances but the practice was discontinued for various reasons. With regard to the impact of adoption of NET, the management is of the view that since the university has used state-of-the-art technologies since it was founded, it is difficult to evaluate the impact.

Private universities

Northcap University

The university stated that usage of NET was limited in traditional undergraduate courses, while in engineering courses it was used extensively, followed by other courses such as management, law and research programmes. The university uses in-house developed and proprietary software in addition to open source software. Being a private university, the decision to use NET is taken by the university management and teachers. The initiatives of management and teachers are found to be the main motivating factors in NET usage. The management is confident that the NET initiatives taken by the institution are sustainable. In fact they have future plans to make recorded lectures available to students through LMS. As far as the upgradation of the knowledge base of faculty members in using the latest NET is concerned, in-house training and MOOCs are the preferred mode. In addition, financial incentives are also offered to encourage the use of latest teaching technologies. The management felt that they have been able to attract more qualified faculty due to extensive use of NET.

Ansal University

The software used in the university is either in-house developed or proprietary. The management feels that students prefer online teaching. The head of the departments have full liberty to decide the type of new technologies to be used in the classrooms. The initiative of teachers and students are found to be the main motivating factors in adoption of NET. The institution did not find any difficulty in implementing the new technologies. The university finds that NET initiatives are very much sustainable. The faculty is encouraged to use latest technologies by providing financial incentives. Specialized IT firms are invited to upgrade the understanding of faculty on latest developments in the field of teaching methods. On the impact of adoption of NET, the institution feels that the strength of students has increased substantially and they have been able to attract more qualified faculty.

Symbiosis International University

The adoption of NET in academic activities is very high in this university. The entire library resources are completely online. In addition to class notes, the teachers ensures that the syllabus and reading materials are available online. It was reported that faculty uses a standalone system rather than an online system for teaching in the class. This is because the students prefer to use standalone systems. However, the students prefer to submit project reports by both online as well as offline methods. The university has installed a software system called 'Turnitin' to control plagiarism. It was found that NET is heavily used in management courses. The centre prefers to use proprietary software systems rather than in-house developed or open source software. Like many institutions, the decision to use NET for teaching rests with the concerned teacher, though initiatives of management are considered most important. The NET use is to some extent also influenced by competitive pressure. The initiative and appreciation of students also influences the extent of use of digital technologies.

On the question of the sustainability of digital technologies used, the management feels that such initiatives are very much sustainable. One of the factors in sustaining these technologies is the faculty upgradation programmes, which helps faculty to acquire up-to-date knowledge of teaching technologies. In this context, the university regularly sends faculty to other institutions under faculty upgradation programme. At times administrative instruments are also used to motivate faculty for awareness of new teaching technologies. The institute did not find any impediments in implementing digital technologies. The management reported that they could attract more qualified faculty due to adoption of NET.

References

Johnson, T., Wisniewski, M. A., Kuhlemeyer, G., Isaacs, G. M., & Krzykowski, J. (2012). Technology adoption in higher education: Overcoming anxiety through faculty bootcamp. *Journal of Asynchronous Learning Networks*, 16(2), 63–72.

Suliman, A. A. E., Fie, D. Y. G., Raman, M., & Alam, N. (2008). Barriers for implementing ICT on higher education in underdeveloped countries: 'Sudan: Case Study'. *CONF-IRM 2008 Proceedings*. Retrieved from https://pdfs.semanticscholar.org/b27d/3baec29b02b6ab74f40de973c8cb4a25f1eb.pdf.

Valcke, M. (2003). Promoting innovation through ICT in Higher Education: Case study Flanders. In M. van der Wende & M. van de Ven (Eds.), *ICT in Higher Education: A Mirror of Europe* (pp. 163–180). Dordrecht: Kluwer.

7 Summary and policy implications

This chapter presents comparative analysis from the viewpoint of the financial nature of the institutions in the study. The financial nature of the institution has implications for management, appointment of faculty, their service conditions and also provision of NET that in turn affects the penetration of digital technologies. A comparison is also made with regard to the intensity of digital technologies used by the students in all types of institutions. Finally, policy implications are also drawn based on the study.

Comparative analysis

The findings of the study were based on 201 students and 43 faculty members of seven universities located in NCR. The students were grouped into three categories based on the intensity of their NET use. It was found that, although NET infrastructure was found to be better in private universities, a higher percentage of students in the extensive users category came from public-funded institutions. The main purposes for which digital technology is used are downloading of reading material and preparation of assignments. Neither students nor faculty prefer the use of e-classroom technologies. The study concluded that use of NET in understanding concepts more clearly, better illustration of ideas and convenience of managing academic activities is found to be highly relevant. The majority of the students reported that the visible impacts of NET use are better communication and collaboration with classmates, skill development and greater control of class activities. The study also found that the facility to share and read students' materials online, as well as submit assignments online, contributed to the learning process.

It can be inferred from the anecdotal evidence collected from the individual universities that the nature of institution influences the degree of NET use. For instance, availability of Wi-Fi is limited in public universities while in private universities the entire campuses are Wi-Fi enabled. There are various factors behind this phenomenon. First, the decision-making process and access to financial resources needed are very different. It is very fast in private universities and extremely archaic in public universities. The time lag and availability of funds from the government always remains a problem. On the other hand, in private universities, these bottlenecks do not exist. Their management can acquire need-based technologies as and when they are required.

The competition among private universities is another factor that compels them to remain up to date in technological advancements. Private universities report that having the most up-to-date technology helps them to attract more students and qualified faculty. Although the management in private universities did not report it, there is always pressure on teachers to adopt the latest teaching technologies. One thing that has emerged as the same in both types of institutions is that students still prefer to use stand-alone systems for teaching. With regards to the impact of NET, all types of institutions have acknowledged that adoption of new technologies contributes to better quality teaching and research.

It may be inferred from the opinion of the management of these institutions that use of NET is very high in managerial functions and limited in academic activities. It was reported that digital technologies are being more extensively used in engineering and IT-related courses but are very limited in traditional courses.

With respect to comparative analysis of faculty, it was found that the percentage of female teachers in private universities is much higher than that of public universities. The age distribution of faculty suggests that they are much younger in public-new and private universities. The analysis of faculty data suggests that institutions are gender-biased as far as teachers are concerned. Private universities prefer more female faculty while more male teachers are found to be employed in public-funded universities. As far as Wi-Fi availability on campus is concerned, the behaviour of public-new and private institutions is the same. Their entire campuses are found to be Wi-Fi enabled, while in public-funded institutions only individual departments are. This situation may be attributed to the size of campuses of the institutions.

An analysis of the opinion of teachers on the mode of teaching suggests that most teachers across all the institutions preferred teaching in an offline mode, i.e. using whiteboards. This may be partially attributed to the preference of students. It was found during the survey that the majority of students, other than engineering students, preferred the offline mode of teaching rather than Internet or intranet-based teaching. By comparing other modes of teaching in various types of institutions, the study found that NET use in teaching is higher in private and public-new universities than in public ones. As a consequence of this, the classrooms are found to be equipped with whiteboards in all the universities. However, the classrooms in public-new and private universities were equipped with modern technologies such as Internet and intranet as well, which was missing to a great extent in public-funded universities.

Opinions of motivational factors for greater diffusion of modern teaching technologies were collected and analysed. The analysis suggested that self-motivation and expectations of students emerged as the major factors and were found to be similar across all the universities. In addition, the faculty of public-new and private universities reported that ease of explaining concepts is another motivating factor in NET use, while importance was placed on ease of managing class notes by faculty of all the institutions. The study revealed that Internet browsing is performed by teachers on a daily basis in all the sample institutions. It was also reported by the respondents that faculty use digital technologies for preparing digital lectures and exercises and tasks for students once per week.

On the question of acquisition and upgradation of knowledge about new teaching technologies, it is ascertained that learning by doing was found to be the best way to acquire knowledge for effective teaching. However, the teachers were also of the view that subject-specific training is also helpful in knowledge acquisition. On the role of management in promotion of NET use, the teachers across all the institutions felt that faculty development initiatives were the best that could be supported by the management. Respondents from public-new and private universities reported that job promotion initiatives could also be an instrument in the promotion of NET use by management.

It was perceived that there could be impediments that may affect the diffusion of NET. Both stream- and institution-specific obstacles were included in the analysis. Among the stream-specific obstacles, the irrelevance of too many digital technologies is cited as one of the reasons for lower use of digital technologies in the social sciences. On the issue of institutional impediments, no one factor was defined as a major obstacle in the diffusion of digital technologies. Factors such as 'inappropriate ICT infrastructure in the institution' and 'unreliable ICT infrastructure' were considered as obstacles to some extent. We may also infer from the findings that the state government is quite vigilant in providing appropriate bandwidth and consequently the speed of communication was not reported as a major obstacle in the use of NET.

Policy implications

One of the objectives of the study was to identify the role of the state in promoting the diffusion of NET. This was thought of as necessary because an external factor such as network technology is beyond the control of HEIs and therefore the state may have a role to play. Although communication networks are fully privatized in India and there are many players in the field, they still need the support of the state in the form of accessing satellite bandwidth. In the Indian context, the launching and management of satellites is still in the hands of the government. For effective use of digital technologies, access to appropriate bandwidth is extremely important and this is where the state plays a very vital role in promoting the use of digital technologies in academic institutions.

Access to bandwidth is a highly dynamic phenomenon because institutions require higher bandwidth to meet the increased use of applications. Therefore one policy implication is that government should remain watchful and provide appropriate bandwidth so that educational institutions can access appropriate bandwidth in order to ensure more integrated NET.

The second policy implication is that universities should be encouraged to conduct regular capacity-building programmes to ensure that the teaching fraternity is not only well informed about new technologies but also they can use these technologies and reap their benefits. In the process, students will also benefit. The study in this book found that the use of NET is very limited in academic activities. Orientation programmes will help faculty to use digital technologies in teaching also on a par with global academic institutions.

Appendix I

HEIs at a glance

Table AI.1 HEIs at a glance

Year	*2011–2012*	*2012–2013*	*2013–2014*	*2014–2015*	*2015–2016*
No. of universities	642	667	723	760	799
Annual growth		3.89	8.40	5.12	5.13
No. of colleges	34,852	35,525	36,634	38,498	39,071
Annual growth		1.93	3.12	5.09	1.49
No. of standalone institutions	11,157	11,565	11,664	12,276	11,923
Annual growth		3.66	0.86	5.25	−2.88
Student–teacher ratio*					
All institutions	21	20	21	21	20
University and colleges	21	21	21	22	21
University and its units	16	16	16	15	16

Source: http://aishe.gov.in

Note

* For regular students.

Appendix II

Description of factors

Table AII.1 Description of factors

Factors	*Description*	*Label*
1	Helps in understanding concepts more clearly, contributes to better illustration of ideas, increases creativity, helps with better job prospects, improves learning abilities, provides opportunity to interact with students of other institutions effectively, equates with international teaching methodologies, convenience in use	RELEVANCE 1
2	Better communication and collaboration with classmates, skill development, prompt feedback from the faculty, provides more opportunities for practice and reinforcement, focus on real-world tasks, allows greater control of class activities	IMPACT 1
3	Accountancy, tour and travel, hospitality, auto and auto-component, agro-based industry	JOB 1
4	Accessing library resources, downloading reading material, communicating with other students and friends, to see results	PURPOSE 1
5	Online syllabus, online readings, online discussion board, online sample exams, submitting assignments online, getting back online assignments from faculty with comments	LEARNING 1
6	Preparation of assignment, communicating with teachers, communicating with college/university	PURPOSE 2
7	Mobile-related work, mobile-related training	JOB 2
8	Computer-related work, computer-related training	JOB 3
9	Makes the students more confident, helps in personality development	RELEVANCE 2
10	Medical profession, journalism, food processing	JOB 4
11	Online sharing of material among students	LEARNING 2
12	Helpful in managing class activities	RELEVANCE 3
13	Downloading class notes	PURPOSE 3

Appendix III

Student questionnaire

A Demographics – personal

1 Name of College/University: ____________________
2 Location of College/University: NCR ☐ Delhi ☐
3 Address of College/University: ____________________
____
____
4 Name of the Student: ____________________
5 Gender: Male ☐ Female ☐
6 Age group: 18–20 ☐ 21–23 ☐ 24+ ☐
7 Course pursuing:
  i Traditional arts and commerce courses (BA, BCom, MA, MCom) ☐
  ii Traditional science courses (BSc, MSc) ☐
  iii Professional courses (Nursing, Media studies, ICT-related) ☐
  iv Engineering courses (BTech, BArch, MTech etc.) ☐
  v Management courses ☐
  vi Law ☐
  vii Research (PhD and innovation) ☐
  viii Any other ☐ ____________________
8 Subject specialization: ____________________
9 Current status of the course: Full time ☐ Part time ☐

B Access of New Educational Technologies (NET)

1 Personal
  i Desktop with Internet ☐
  ii Standalone desktop ☐
  iii Laptop with Internet ☐
  iv Standalone laptop ☐

v Tablet/iPad ☐
vi E-reader ☐

2 Institutional
i Desktop with Internet ☐
ii Standalone desktop ☐
iii Laptop with Internet ☐
iv Standalone laptop ☐
v Tablet/iPad ☐
vi E-reader ☐

3 Do you have access to intranet in your institution? Yes ☐ No ☐

4 Do you have access to Wi-Fi in your institution? Yes ☐ No ☐

5 Does your college/university have cloud computing? Yes ☐ No ☐

6 Indicate the speed of Internet
<100 MBPS ☐ 100 MBPS – <1 GBPS ☐ > = 1 GBPS ☐

7 Extent of use of NET
i No use of NET ☐
ii Limited use (e-mails, Internet, limited use for class) ☐
iii Moderate use (ii and online activities) ☐
iv Extensive use (iii and most of the class activities online) ☐

8 Purpose of use of digital technologies
i Preparation of assignment ☐
ii Access to library resources ☐
iii Download reading material ☐
iv Download class notes ☐
v Communication with teachers ☐
vi Comm. with other students/friends ☐
vii Communication with your college/university ☐
viii To see results ☐
ix Any other ☐ ______________________

C Impact and impediments of using NET

1 Which of the following benefits from using digital technology in the class was most relevant to you?
(Choose on a 4-point scale: 1 'Not useful', 2 'Neutral', 3 'Useful', 4 'Very useful')
i Helped in understanding concepts more clearly ☐
ii Better illustration of ideas ☐
iii Increased creativity ☐
iv Better job prospects ☐
v Made more confident ☐
vi Helped in personality development ☐

vii Improved my learning abilities ☐
viii Provides opportunity to interact with students of other institutions effectively ☐
ix Equated with international teaching methodologies ☐
x Convenience ☐
xi Helped in managing my class activities (e.g. planning, apportioning time etc.) ☐
xii Any other ☐______________________________

2 To what extent the use of ICT has helped you in the following aspects?
(Choose on 5-point scale: 1 'Strongly disagree', 2 'Disagree', 3 'Neutral', 4 'Agree', 5 'Strongly agree')
i Helped me to better communicate with faculty ☐
ii Helped me to better communicate and collaborate with class mates ☐
iii Helped me in skill development ☐
iv Has resulted in prompt feedback from the faculty ☐
v Provides more opportunities for practice and reinforcement ☐
vi More likely to focus on real-world tasks and examples ☐
vii Allows greater control of my class activities (e.g. planning, apportioning time) ☐

3 How did the following help you to improve learning or managing classes?
(Choose on a 4-point scale: 1 'Do not use', 2 'Negative effect', 3 'No effect', 4 'Improved learning')
i Online syllabus ☐
ii Online readings ☐
iii Online discussion board ☐
iv Online access to sample exams ☐
v Submitting assignments online ☐
vi Getting online assignments back from faculty with comments ☐
vii Online sharing material among students ☐

4 What are the barriers for using e-classes?
(Rate on a 4-point scale: 1 'Not at all', 2 'To some extent', 3 'Moderate', 4 'Major barrier')
i Not very relevant ☐
ii Don't have necessary skills ☐
iii Don't have technical support needed ☐
iv E-class infra is insufficient ☐
v E-classes are not very effective ☐
vi Technology is not very reliable ☐

5 Indicate the type of job you prefer
(Rank choices as: 1 'most preferred' and 14 'least preferred')

i Computer-related work ☐
ii Accountancy ☐
iii Computer-related training ☐
iv Tour and travel ☐
v Mobile-related work ☐
vi Hospitality ☐
vii Mobile-related training ☐
viii Auto and auto-component ☐
ix Medical profession ☐
x Agro-based industry ☐
xi Journalism ☐
xii Food processing ☐
xiii Coaching institute ☐
xiv Any other ☐___________________________

Appendix IV

Teacher questionnaire

A Demographic information of respondent

1 Name of College/University: ____________________

2 Name of Respondent: ____________________

3 Gender: Male ☐ Female ☐ 3.1. Age group: <30 ☐ 30–44 ☐ 45+ ☐

4 Designation: Assistant Professor ☐ Associate Professor ☐ Professor ☐

5 Subjects taught: ____________ Faculty: ____________

6 Job status: Part time ☐ Full time ☐

7 Work experience: 1–5 years ☐ 6–10 years ☐ >10 years ☐

8 Is the campus Wi-Fi enabled? Yes ☐ No ☐

If No, rank the following reasons on 5-point scale, 1'least important' to 5 'most important'

- i Uneconomical ☐
- ii No reasonable demand ☐
- iii Connectivity to satellite is not reliable ☐
- iv Any other ☐

9 Does the campus have intranet? Yes ☐ No ☐

If No, rank the following reasons on 5-point scale, 1'least important' to 5 'most important'

- i Uneconomical ☐
- ii No reasonable demand ☐
- iii Connectivity to network is not reliable ☐
- iv Any other ☐

B Intensity of ICT use

1 Mode of teaching in class

- i Online (institution server) ☐
- ii Internet ☐
- iii Standalone ☐
- iv Traditional ☐

2 Is your classroom equipped with?
   i Standalone computer ☐
   ii Computer with Internet access ☐
   iii Computer with intranet access ☐
   iv Whiteboard ☐
   v Blackboard ☐

3 Factors that motivated you to use ICTs in teaching
(Please rank the following choices on a 5-point scale, 1 'least important' to 5 'most important')
   i Self-motivation ☐
   ii Management made compulsory ☐
   iii Expectations of students ☐
   iv Ease of explaining the concepts in class ☐
   v Followed other teachers ☐
   vi Encouragement from management ☐
   vii Ease of managing lecture notes ☐
   viii Any other ☐ ______________________________

4 Please rate on a 4-point scale, how often you use the following tools for preparing the lectures
(1 'Rarely', 2 'Twice a month', 3 'Once a week', 4 'Twice a week', 5 'Every day')
   i Browse/search Internet ☐
   ii Prepare digital lectures on standalone system ☐
   iii Prepare digital exercises and tasks for students ☐
   iv Communicate online with parents and students ☐
   v Communicate online with management ☐
   vi Look for online professional development opportunities ☐

C Upgradation and acquisition of ICT skills

Please rank the following choices on a 5-point scale, 1 'least important' to 5 'most important'
   i Learning by doing ☐
   ii Training is/was organized by the institution ☐
   iii Undertaken professional course ☐
   iv Undertaken subject-specific training ☐
   v Any other ☐ ______________________________

D Promotion of ICT use by management Yes ☐ No ☐

If No, go to E
Please rank the following choices on a 5-point scale, 1 ‘least important’ to 5 ‘most important’

i Faculty development initiatives ☐
ii Financial incentives ☐
iii Better job promotion ☐
iv Any other ☐____________________

E Is the extent of ICT use by your institution sustainable? Yes ☐ No ☐

If No, rank the reasons on 5-point scale 1‘least relevant’ to 5 ‘most relevant’

i Intake of students will decline over time ☐
ii Students may not prefer too much technology in teaching ☐
iii Return on investment may not be sustainable ☐
iv Lack of financial resources ☐
iv Any other ☐____________________

F Obstacles to ICT usage

Please rank the following choices on a 5-point scale, 1 ‘least important’ to 5 ‘most important’

i Irrelevance of new technologies in my subject ☐
ii Inadequate familiarity of ICT tools ☐
iii The lack of orientation towards new technologies ☐
iv Increasing age and reluctance to learn new technologies ☐
v Non-availability of skill upgradation programmes in the institution ☐
vi Lack of incentive ☐
vii Lack of appreciation by students ☐
viii Inappropriate ICT infrastructure in the institution ☐
ix Unreliable ICT infrastructure in the institution ☐
x Any other ☐____________________

Appendix V

Management questionnaire

1 Name of College/University: ______________________________

  i Single campus ☐

  ii Multi-campus ☐ ______________________________

2 Name of the respondent: ______________________________

3 Gender: Male ☐ Female ☐

4 Age group: <30 ☐ 30–44 ☐ 45+ ☐

5 Designation: Vice chancellor ☐ Registrar ☐ Principal ☐

  Others ☐ ______________________________

6 Work experience: 1–5 years ☐ 6–10 years ☐ >10 years ☐

7 Date of inception of the institution: ______________________________

8 Courses offered by your institution:

  i Traditional arts and commerce courses (BA, BCom, MA, MCom) ☐

  ii Traditional science courses (BSc, MSc) ☐

  iii Professional courses (Nursing, Media studies, ICT-related) ☐

  iv Engineering courses (BTech, BArch, MTech etc.) ☐

  v Management courses ☐

  vi Law ☐

  vii Research (PhD and innovation) ☐

  viii Any other ☐ ______________________________

9 Number of students:

Courses	*2014–2015*	*At inception*
Traditional arts and commerce courses (BA, BCom, MA, MCom)		
Traditional science courses (BSc, MSc)		
Professional courses (Nursing, Media studies, ICT-related)		
Engineering courses (BTech, BArch, MTech etc.)		
Management courses		
Law		
Research (PhD and innovation)		

10 ICT configuration
  i Is the campus Wi-Fi enabled? Yes ☐ No ☐
    If No, rank the following reasons on 5-point scale, 1'least important' to 5 'most important'
    a Uneconomical ☐
    b No reasonable demand ☐
    c Connectivity to satellite is not reliable ☐
    d Any other ☐ ________________
  ii Is multi-campus connected through intranet? Yes ☐ No ☐ NA ☐
  iii Central server Yes ☐ No ☐
  iv Departmental server Yes ☐ No ☐
  v Cloud computing Yes ☐ No ☐
11 Use of ICTs in following activities
  i Managerial functions
    a Financial management (accounts) ☐ ________________
    b Related to students (online admission, fee payment etc.) ☐
    c Preparation of results ☐
    d e-Records (students, teachers and staff) ☐
    e Student login ☐
    f Evaluation of faculty by students ☐
    g Verification of certificates issued ☐
  ii Academic functions
    a Availability of online library resources ☐ ________________
    b Availability of online syllabus and reading material in detail ☐
    c Availability of online class notes ☐
    d Use of ICT by faculty in class – Standalone ☐ Online ☐ Offline ☐
    e Use of ICT by students – Standalone ☐ Online ☐
    f Preparation of project reports by students – Offline ☐ Online ☐ Standalone ☐
    g Plagiarism check software (e.g. Turnitin software) ☐
12 Indicate the extent of use of ICT in the following courses
  (Choose on 4 pt. scale 1 'not used at all', 2 'limited use', 3 'heavy use', 4 'very heavy use')
  i Traditional arts and commerce courses (BA, BCom, MA, MCom) ☐
  ii Traditional science courses (BSc, MSc) ☐
  iii Professional courses (Nursing, Media studies, ICT-related) ☐
  iv Engineering courses (BTech, BArch, MTech etc.) ☐
  v Management courses ☐
  vi Law ☐
  vii Research (PhD and innovation) ☐

13 How have you developed ICT tools used in institution?
  i In-house ☐
  ii Open source ☐
  iii Proprietary ☐
14 Who decides use of ICT in teaching?
  i Institution ☐
  ii Teacher ☐
  iii Dean/HOD ☐
15 Preference of students regarding mode of teaching
  i Standalone ☐
  ii Offline ☐
  iii Online ☐
16 Preference of students regarding submission of assignments/projects
  i Standalone ☐
  ii Offline ☐
  iii Online ☐
17 Who motivates you to introduce ICT in the institution?
  (Rank the following on 5-point scale 1'least important' to 5 'most important')
  i Management initiative ☐
  ii Competition ☐
  iii Student initiative ☐
  iv Teacher initiative ☐
18 Is the extent of ICT use by your institution sustainable? Yes ☐ No ☐
  If No, rank the factors on 5-point scale 1'least relevant' to 5 'most relevant'
  i Intake of students will decline over time ☐
  ii Students may not prefer too much technology in teaching ☐
  iii Return on investment may not be sustainable ☐
  iv Lack of financial resources ☐
  v Any other ☐ ____________________
19 How do you motivate teachers to be aware of new teaching technologies?
  i Regular training
    a Inviting IT firms ____________________
    b Sending faculty outside ____________________
    c In-house training (MOOCs) ____________________
  ii Financial incentives ____________________
  iii Administrative instruments ____________________
20 Did you face any hindrance in adoption of new technologies? Yes ☐ No ☐

____

____

21 Impact of adoption of NET
   i Strength of student have increased □
   ii Strength of student have remained same □
   iii Could attract more qualified faculty □
   iv No impact on faculty □

Any other discussion related to adoption of new technologies

____

____

____

____

Index

Page numbers in **bold** denote tables, those in *italics* denote figures.